COLLINS' ILLUSTRATED
ATLAS OF LONDON

THE VICTORIAN LIBRARY

COLLINS' ILLUSTRATED
ATLAS OF LONDON

WITH AN INTRODUCTION BY
H.J.DYOS

LEICESTER UNIVERSITY PRESS
NEW YORK: HUMANITIES PRESS
1973

First published in 1854
Victorian Library edition published in 1973 by
Leicester University Press

Distributed in North America by
Humanities Press Inc., New York

Introduction copyright © Leicester University Press 1973

Printed in Great Britain by
Unwin Brothers Limited, The Gresham Press
Old Woking, Surrey

ISBN 0 7185 5012 9

THE VICTORIAN LIBRARY

There is a growing demand for the classics of Victorian literature in many fields, in political and social history, architecture, topography, religion, education, and science. Hitherto this demand has been met, in the main, from the second-hand market. But the prices of second-hand books are rising sharply, and the supply of them is very uncertain. It is the object of this series, THE VICTORIAN LIBRARY, to make some of these classics available again at a reasonable cost. Since most of the volumes in it are reprinted photographically from the first edition, or another chosen because it has some special value, an accurate text is ensured. Each work carries a substantial introduction, written specially for this series by a well-known authority on the author or his subject, and a bibliographical note on the text.

The volumes necessarily vary in size. In planning the newly-set pages the designer, Arthur Lockwood, has maintained a consistent style for the principal features. The uniform design of binding and jackets provides for ready recognition of the various books in the series when shelved under different subject classifications.

Recommendation of titles for THE VICTORIAN LIBRARY and of scholars to contribute the introductions is made by a joint committee of the Board of the University Press and the Victorian Studies Centre of the University of Leicester.

INTRODUCTION*

Monstrous, marvellous, prodigious London, –
Thou giant city, – mighty in thy size and power,
Surpassing all that was, or is, or may be.
> From the title-page of [John Britton],
> *Picture of London* (26th edn, 1829)

"In the presence of London, it is just as it would be if you should meet a man fifty feet high . . . You would be in a state of perpetual astonishment." The words come from an obscure contributor to a family magazine, writing shortly before this little volume was first published,[1] but they express an attitude that was universal. "The extension of the metropolis of the British empire", declared the *Gentleman's Magazine*, "is one of the marvels of the last century",[2] – a multiplication of numbers, an "elasticity" and "expansibility" that was "almost oppressively palpable", that outdid all the capitals of Europe and was barely overtaken in the public mind by the gold-rushing growth of San Francisco.[3] "London has not grown", complained one writer in *Household Words*, "in any natural, reasonable, understandable way . . . it has swollen with frightful, alarming, supernatural rapidity. It has taken you unawares; it has dropped upon you without warning; it has started up without notice; it has grown with stealthy rapidity, from a mouse into a mastodon."[4]

* I am grateful to Mr V.R.Belcher, Research Assistant to the *Survey of London*, for first introducing me to this work and to Mr. H.O.Wilson, Librarian of the Members' Library, both of the Greater London Council, for making a copy of it available for reprinting.

It had in fact multiplied only two and a half times in about two and a half generations, measured in London terms. In 1801 London was on the verge of becoming the world's first million-peopled city and its rate of growth since then had been exceeded by several northern industrial towns, but what so fascinated those watching was London's insatiable appetite for people. At the beginning of the nineteenth century the area later defined as the Metropolitan Police District – Greater London no less – already contained about 12 per cent of the population of England and Wales; by mid-century the figure was 15 per cent; at its close 20 per cent. On his second visit to London in 1847 Ralph Waldo Emerson had observed that "the nation sits in the immense city they have builded, a London extended into every man's mind."[5]

The convergence there of all the major institutions in the nation's life – the crown, parliament, government, law, commerce, industry, finance, fashion – had long provided the ingredients for the national fixation of the times: that London represented not so much the apex of provincial life as a funnel for its wealth and its people.[6] Thomas de Quincey, who started life in Manchester, had often felt its powerful suction, he said, since first visiting London as a youth for a day in 1800 – a suction that was "operating, night and day, summer and winter, and hurrying for ever into one centre the infinite means needed for her infinite purposes, and the endless tributes to the skill or to the luxury of her endless population. . . ."[7] Not surprisingly, Coleridge had called London the "Leviathan", Cobbett the "Wen", Robert Mudie "Babylon the Great", Emerson "the Rome of to-day", and to the widening circle of writers who, in the 1830s and 1840s, were offering themselves as pathfinders along its secret ways, it was a vast and mysterious continent demanding to be explored.[8] "Let us roll out the map of London", wrote one of them, "and

take a glance at its terrible physiology. These fine streets that we trace are but the frontier of a kingdom of which the upper classes know as little as of the interior of Japan."[9] Even a Londoner as knowledgeable as Sala had left great tracts untouched. No-one from Stowe to Dickens – no, not Pepys nor Maitland – had done more, he thought, than scratch the surface of London. "I never travelled in London", he wrote in 1857, "though I am a cockney born . . . I candidly confess that I never was in Bethnal Green in my life, that I have a very indistinct notion of the latitude of Hackney, that I don't know where Bluegate Fields are situated." He must, he said, "construe this metropolitan Abracadabra . . . read this Rosetta inscription."[10] What we can sense here is a consciousness of the city as *terra incognita*, a man-made wilderness more daunting than tropical forests, more inscrutable than the Sahara. London was in truth a place with a regional geography of its own; it was a globe to itself: "behold, within the Arctic circle the migratory Esquimaux of Camden Town," declared John Fisher Murray; ". . . the Australasian territories of our southern metropolitan hemisphere."[11]

Here, indeed, was a place into which it was inconceivable that anyone, visitor or native, dare go unaided: a map was indispensable; an atlas might be better. When *Collins' Illustrated Atlas of London* offered itself for the second time, in 1859, it was "as a guide and friend to all who seek for information through the labyrinths of the Metropolis." Collins's was not in fact the first street guide to London to describe itself as an atlas – a term hitherto kept for collections of maps of some territorial substance.[12] The distinction of first putting London on such a par belongs to James Wyld the younger, who had assumed his father's style as Geographer to the Queen and H.R.H. Prince Albert and produced five or six years before *An Atlas of London & its Environs*, a portfolio of

eight sheets measuring almost four feet square. This was something to be deliberated over, and never out of doors. *Collins' Illustrated Atlas*, on the other hand, was the first street guide specifically designed to go into the pocket and to be consulted under all street conditions, its plates being specially drawn for it, and every street that could be found being listed in it.

It had been a matter of commonsense since the 1760s to fit fairly large-scale maps for the pocket simply by folding them sufficiently and carrying them in a slip-case, and this practice did not begin to change before about 1830.[13] Most maps of London produced in this period had fallen into two categories: small-scale maps of less than one inch to the mile encompassing a radius of around 15 miles of Charing Cross; large-scale maps upwards of four inches or so to the mile and covering the continuously built-up area to its limits. The second group was about twice as large as the first. About half of these larger-scale maps were either cut into sections or mounted for folding (almost all the smaller-scale maps were designed to be kept flat) and it was a natural step sooner or later to bind up maps prepared in this way into the form of a book. Cruchley's *Environs of London*, drawn to a scale of nearly five inches to the mile and first issued in a slip-case in 1825 or 1826, was presented in 1830, as its cartouche announced, "bound in a novel form as a book". There was an extra innovation because it included a paginated index to the streets and principal places of interest. Since fairly early in the eighteenth century the principal street names were usually listed in the margins of so-called 'pocket maps' and 'city guides' and such maps were divided into squares for easy reference; sometimes important buildings were numbered and drawn into a decorative frieze, sometimes interspersed with awesome statistics. One idea was to provide a gazetteer in a booklet pasted inside the outer cover of a folding case. This was an advance on a

much older idea used by Ogilby and Morgan as long before as 1677 in their *London Survey'd: or, an Explanation of the Large Map of London*, which was simply an index to the great survey of London they had completed following the Fire;[14] Rocque's plan of 1746 had also been augmented a year later by a substantial index of a similar kind;[15] Horwood's plan, too, was very effectively indexed; but perhaps the most developed form of index was that supplied as a *Companion* to Langley & Belch's *New Map of London* (1812), which ran to 172 pages. Although Cruchley's book-like plan of 1830 combined these possibilities in what now seems a most ingenious and convenient way, the idea failed to catch on: Deacon's small-scale map of the environs of London to a distance of 30 miles, published in 1831, was apparently its only imitator.

By the 1850s mapmaking had become all the same a notoriously derivative business. The six maps shown at the Great Exhibition in 1851 were versions of maps that had been available for anything up to 60 years, perhaps even more.[16] Advances were being made, for the trigonometrical survey of the country which had been started in 1784 had led to the publication of the one-inch Ordnance Survey for the four counties impinging on London in the years 1805–22, and its measurements must have passed fairly rapidly into the stock-in-trade of commercial mapmakers. More important for basic urban engineering was the completion, in 1851, of the central portion of the much larger-scale survey being conducted, on the double scale of five feet and 12 inches to the mile, at the instigation of the Metropolitan Commission of Sewers in 1847 – though the whole thing was not completed till 1871.[17]

In the meantime a vast but cruder stock of more easily adapted material was at hand to meet the growing demand of people visiting London who merely wanted to be able to find their way about. Richard Horwood's meticulous though

imperfect survey, completed on a scale of 26 inches to the mile in 1792–9 covering the whole area between Islington and Kensington, Limehouse and Brompton, provided one such base. The conscientiously up-dated editions of John Cary's *New and Accurate Plan*, first issued in 1787, covering approximately the same extent but on a scale of 6½ inches to the mile, was another; and the scarcely less authentic and beautifully engraved maps of William Faden, Christopher and John Greenwood, George Cruchley, and James Wyld (both father and son), and of one or two others besides, provided an abundant source for copyists, not to say one another, during the first half of the nineteenth century. The old plates were often handed down – as Horwood's were to Faden and then to Wyld – though this did not necessarily imply a failure to update the original version, and in this case thorough revision of a map of the City first issued in 1780 makes his edition of 1840 unusually valuable. However, sometimes the original plates were neither re-etched nor revised so carefully, even by the reputable mapmakers, and these occasionally became fuzzy or hopelessly outdistanced by the proliferating suburbs.[18]

Henry George Collins was one among many mapmakers and mapsellers who rose on the great tourist tide that engulfed London during and immediately following the exhibitions of 1851 and 1862. The market was a very large one. Over six million people were admitted to the Great Exhibition during the long season of 1851 (it was dismantled in 1852 and reopened at Sydenham in June 1854, ten days after *Collins' Atlas* appeared). The great aim of the publicists was to make London itself an exhibition out-of-doors, a public show requiring the entrance fee merely of the price of a pocket map – something to be understood, used, enjoyed, and finally disposed of. This was a time when old maps appeared unashamedly in disguise and new editions could masquerade

under new names. James Reynolds' four-inch map of 1847, for example, already replete with a guide for viewing the "sights and amusements of London" as a six days' wonder, merely needed redating 1851, the whereabouts of the Exhibition marked and tinted, and a new label affixed to the cover to become *The Exhibition Map of London*.

Novelty was inclined to breed novelty. The 'distance map' had a brief vogue following the publication of J.Friederichs' *The Circuiteer* about 1847, on which a continuous grid of half-mile circles was superimposed with the idea of making it easy to decide whether to walk or take a cab. John Tallis's highly original idea of providing "a complete stranger's guide through London" by means of a series of detailed elevations to the main streets, coupled with street directories, views of the principal buildings, and miniature street maps, had also reappeared in 1847.[19] *A Balloon View of London* covering eight square miles as seen from an altitude of a thousand feet above Hampstead Heath appeared in 1851. Skeleton maps that enabled the visitor to find without seeking, as in Virtue & Co.'s *The British Metropolis in 1851*, cut through the bewildering detail in another way. The *Post Office Directory* map – the best cheap map of London according to Murray's[20] – came supplied in the 1855 edition with a patent index and a tape affixed to one edge for locating the place names.

Collins' Illustrated Atlas was something of a novelty, too. Unlike almost all other maps of London ever known, each of its 36 sections was oriented on a different axis from the others, the sub-division of the ground being determined largely by the direction taken by the main thoroughfares between St Paul's and the suburbs but partly by the whimsical desire to stand the visitor, or the town, on their heads: the top of every map pointed in a different direction and every one overlapped the adjoining sheets all round – St Paul's appeared

on six of them. Turning the map sideways or upside-down to get one's bearings was supposedly unnecessary. There was some resemblance here to the maps in *Tallis's London Street Views*, which not only disregarded the compass completely but often inverted the street names in an effort to square up with the views themselves. The *Atlas*'s size permitted it, the introduction pointed out, to be used "without notice or inconvenience of any kind". (The vertical margins have been slightly increased in this edition, to accommodate the maps more comfortably.) Anyone unwilling to abandon the notion that the north is always uppermost must nevertheless have been driven to distraction.

This may help to explain why Collins himself did not last long as a mapseller. He disappeared within a decade. His first publication had been a small-scale map of London and its environs in 1851 and the following year he produced his *Pocket Ordnance Railway Atlas of Great Britain*. With some prescience he brought out in 1853 a map of Russia and Turkey and, when hostilities began in the Crimea the year after, put another half-a-dozen local charts and plans of the theatre of war on sale. He also produced two or three more railway maps. Very shortly after he had gone into partnership with his brother, Henry Edward Collins, and William Paprill in 1858 or 1859 the firm went bankrupt. His last publication seems to have been an *Indestructible Atlas of the Earth* [1858]. The edition of the *Illustrated Atlas of London* that appeared in 1859 was published instead by Thomas Hodgson and that of 1862 by Darton & Hodge.[21]

It is clear from the plates themselves that they were not lithographic transfers from any existing map, though the claim that they were based on an independent survey must remain rather more open. The vignetted views bear a fugitive resemblance to some of the numerous engravings to be found in

near-contemporary guide books – *Cruchley's Picture Book of London* (1846) offers two or three more positive likenesses – but it is hard to justify these suspicions. As for the street plan itself, it must be admitted that it would have been straight-forward enough to take it straight off a number of existing maps. The inclination to block in back streets and courts to a greater extent than most contemporary maps on the same scale did tends to diminish somewhat the claim that a survey was taken specially. The scale used was $3\frac{3}{4}$ inches to the mile, the same as that of Cruchley's famous *New Plan of London in Miniature* [1827] and Wyld's *Atlas of London & its Environs* [1848–9] – the first covering a rather smaller area and the second a much larger one than Collins's – and there had been a score of such maps published in the previous 40 years, a number of them even distributed gratis with periodicals like the *Railway Bell and Illustrated London Advertiser* (1845) and the *United Kingdom Newspaper* (1832). Of Richard Jarman, the engraver of *Collins' Illustrated Atlas*, little is known beyond the fact that he also produced a map of Portsmouth and Southsea about 1865.

Despite the perverse arrangement of the plates, the *Atlas* had the great merit of imposing a rational order of some kind on London's apparently meaningless geography: it made the mass manageable. Though it covered not very much more than a third of London as delimited by the Registrar-General for census purposes, it included all but a fraction of the 40 or 50 square miles of its continuously built-up area and upwards of three-quarters of its total population of around $2\frac{1}{2}$ millions. The line of the North London Railway, which traversed all the most northerly plates, roughly defined the built-up limits on that side, just as the line of the New Road had done up to 40 years before and the Regent's Canal until the last 20 years. Beyond it, settlement was still fairly scattered,

concentrated for the most part on villages not yet overtaken by the urban ooze. Down river, where Bromley and Bow and, more conspicuously, Poplar had opened salients across the lower Lea valley, and in a series of northerly uphill thrusts into Dalston, Islington, Kentish Town, and Kilburn, the growth points of the next ten or 20 years were already forming. Beyond the congested corner of the flood plain on the other bank the settlement was much looser and indeterminate: a great band of half-formed suburbs dotted across the higher ground between Blackheath, Denmark Hill, Brixton, and Wandsworth.

The *Atlas* stopped a good way short of most of these newer places, but the direction in which it might be said to have stopped altogether too abruptly was in the west, especially towards Notting Hill and Kensington, which were beginning to grow fast. These limitations apart, it had kept up well with developments closer to the centre: the Great Western Railway's new Paddington terminus on Praed Street, for example, which had not been opened till 1854, was duly shown; impending developments like the new cattle market in the Caledonian Road (opened in 1855) and Battersea Park (laid out and planted in 1856–7) were correctly indicated; the limits of the open ground were accurately shown. With one major exception, no change of any consequence of the previous decade had been overlooked.

The exception is the railway system. This also rather tells against the *Atlas* as an independent survey but it is something of a puzzle in itself because the canals are all shown, as the railway termini are ("recent and novel creations", as one writer had lately put it, "that as yet are in, but scarcely of, London"[22]), and the lines themselves were added to the 1859 edition. The railways were neither inconspicuous on the ground nor insignificant in their operation, especially where

they were carried on those long brick viaducts that marked the street plan so indelibly.

Yet it is important to remember how small a presence the railway had made within the central area as such by the 1850s. The lines built in the 1830s and 1840s had, with the exception of the Blackwall Railway, merely come to the edge of the built-up area and had not pierced it. From the mid-1840s till the end of the 1850s the railway was deliberately barred from central London: indeed, the bulk of its railway system, perforce a suburban one, did not come into being before the 1860s and 1870s. It was then that the railway became for a time a weapon of destruction, as lines that had been devised after the ground had been taken for houses and other buildings plunged remorselessly among them.[23] The *Atlas* belongs to the intervening lull, when the streets were virtually the only avenues of communication, when their superstructures were in form and substance largely an inheritance of the pre-Victorian past, and when London itself remained an inveterate, if diverting, obstacle to through travel between North and South.

The streets offered obstacles of their own. Despite the supposed abolition 25 years earlier, at the instigation of the Metropolitan Turnpike Commission, of the road tolls north of the river, there were within four miles of Charing Cross in the 1850s more gates and bars still standing than there had been in 1830, despite a well-packed lobby at Westminster to oppose them.[24] They were thickest on the ground in Notting Hill, Kentish Town, Holloway, Stamford Hill, Hackney, Peckham, and Camberwell, and their virtual abolition did not come until 1865.[25] At the same time only London, Blackfriars and Westminster Bridges (the last newly built) were free of toll, and the other four – excepting Hungerford, which was a footbridge – were not completely cleared of theirs before 1879

(when the Chelsea, Albert, and Battersea Bridges were also cleared, leaving only Wandsworth, Putney, and Hammersmith to be made toll-free the following year). The *Illustrated London News* calculated in 1854 that, what with the toll and other inconveniences, "five-sixths of the whole traffic of the largest city in the civilised world pours over one bridge".[26]

London was not all it might have been, and there was a faint but increasingly nagging implication in remarks like this that the beautification of Paris, which was going ahead with such style and resolution, was a reproach on London. *Punch* was often carping about such things: "Paris making such a movement in her buildings and her streets, How is it that all improvement here with opposition meets?"[27] The more London grew, grumbled the *Illustrated London News*, the more unwholesome it was becoming: "The new London of Belgravia and Tyburnia may stand comparison for beauty and splendour with any city in the world; but old London and Westminster, with their outlying boroughs of Southwark, Lambeth, the Tower Hamlets, and Finsbury, have positively nothing to recommend them but wealth, extent, and populousness." In Chancery Lane, the only direct connection between the parallel westward thoroughfares of Fleet Street and the Strand on one side and of Holborn and New Oxford Street on the other, the traffic was often brought to a standstill, it contemptuously declared, by a laundress's wheelbarrow.[28]

The truth of the matter is that the streets of London remained in 1854 roughly in the condition they had been 20 or 30 years before. A more sobering truth is that the road system of London as a whole scarcely changed, except at three or four crucial spots, over an ensuing period twice as long.

Taking New Oxford Street through the slums of St Giles separating Holborn and Tottenham Court Road in 1847 was

one vital step, but the through-route it promised via Newgate, Cheapside, Cornhill, Aldgate, and Whitechapel was frustrated by the steep and narrow crossing of the Fleet Valley, until Holborn Viaduct swept over it in 1869. The more southerly east-west route had a couple of serious bottlenecks in it, at Temple Bar and Ludgate Hill, but it was prevented from converging on the other route in Cheapside by the extension of Cannon Street straight to St Paul's, an improvement completed just in time for inclusion in the *Atlas*. The City had never been seriously short of outlets to the north save at one point, beyond Holborn Circus, and the scheme to cut a new street to Clerkenwell Green, which had been initiated in 1832 as a means of extending Farringdon Street, was still incomplete when the *Atlas* appeared: it reached Bagnigge Wells Road (now King's Cross Road) in 1856 and was named Farringdon Road (having first been known as Victoria Street).

The only other major new streets to be imposed on central London in the 60 years after publication of the *Atlas* are the two constellations of Charing Cross Road-Shaftesbury Avenue (1886–7) and Theobalds Road-Clerkenwell Road-Rosebery Avenue (1878–1902), the Albert, Victoria and Chelsea Embankments (1868–74), Southwark Street (1862–4), and Kingsway (1905). Victoria Street, Westminster (1851), which, like its Clerkenwell namesake, was still being developed when the *Atlas* was published, Queen Victoria Street (1871), and Northumberland Avenue (1876) were all less important as traffic arteries.

What is not possible to discover from this street guide are the means of getting about, the way the city functioned, or the elements of its social geography.[29] What we have, apart from the maps, is a solemn enough roll-call of government buildings, almshouses, asylums, breweries, cemeteries, churches, hospitals, monuments, markets, prisons, and the like, along with a

brief flourish of theatres, pleasure gardens, museums, galleries, waxworks, and peepshows of varying pretensions. It is not a complete list. Most obviously perhaps, it omits the recently-established music halls and casinos, the widening range of hotels, clubs, shops and arcades, and necessarily offers few hints of that other London which became the subject of books like J.Ewing Ritchie's *The Night Side of London* (1857) or *London in the Sixties* (1908) by "One of the Old Brigade". The frivolities – and the miseries – of Victorian London constitute a whole library of their own.

On a more mundane level, the *Atlas* did not explain how to get about this bedevilling place. It offered no rules of thumb for reckoning cab fares – three shillings would take one almost anywhere – nor guidance on where to catch a bus or how much it would cost, but these mostly ran through the City or the West End and out to the suburbs so frequently and cheaply – sixpence or less all the way – while their service and direction were so mercurial that no comprehensive route map was ever offered to the general public before the more settled era of the London Passenger Transport Board's monopoly rule in the 1930s. *Collins' Illustrated Atlas* appeared, as it happened, at a moment of crisis for both the omnibus and coaching businesses: the latter because the railway had so lately driven the long-distance coaches off the roads and with them the business that had sustained the City's coaching inns; the former because, among other things, excessive numbers of buses brought onto the roads to cater for the tourist traffic of 1851 had led to fare-cutting at a time when operating costs were rising – the outbreak of the Crimean War in the spring of 1854 added to these by causing fodder to rise sharply in price. The formation the following year of an undertaking, soon to be known as the London General Omnibus Company, which would exercise a controlling hand over a large part of the omnibus business was

the sequel to this. The tramway was a more distant development.

The mapmaker's is a lifeless art and when applied to such a metropolis supremely so. He can supply no spot check of the human traffic passing through these streets – a mere 26,000 daily commuters, as it happened, in 1854[30] – that will restore their hubbub and incident; he can release none of the sensations of the prodigious daily act of provisioning the city – of close on two million livestock, for instance, being driven on the hoof into Smithfield in weekly instalments, of oxen that might have lined up ten abreast and stretched beyond Peterborough or of sheep all the way to Bristol, or supplied the thought that somewhere among those streets 20,000 cows were stalled up supplying milk.[31] The images he evokes, like those gathered at dawn from the crow's nest erected on the apex of the cross of St Paul's to conduct the Ordnance Survey in 1848, are of an "empire of living mortality . . . Could we unroof the houses and bare to the morning sun the vast congregated population beneath, what a motley, what a painful scene, would be developed."[32]

That sensation of lurking truths about London was being evoked increasingly in the early 1850s. Henry Mayhew's encounters with the secret people of the streets, which were reported to readers of the *Morning Chronicle* in 1849–50 (and have never been repeated *in extenso* since), more than a decade of Dickens's explorations of the terrible interstices in London's familiar façade, the step-by-step accretion of social fact by fascinated statisticians, writings on every level from Max Schlesinger's *Saunterings in and about London* to Charles Manby Smith's *Curiosities of London Life: or, Phases, Physiological and Social, of the Great Metropolis* or John Garwood's *The Million-Peopled City; or, One-half of the people of London made known to the other half* – all of them published the year

before the *Atlas* – and the curiouser and curiouser self-knowledge coming with the censuses (the final report of the 1851 census, the most searching yet, was not published until July 1854) – these were leading, in one direction, to new perceptions of social distance and to a new fashion for slumming, and, in another, to more insistent demands that the amorphous lump be somehow shaped, that the polluting city be somehow cleansed.

What helped to clinch this question was the cholera, which in the course of the summer of 1854 carried off nearly 10,000 souls in London alone: less deadly at large than the visitation of 1849 had been, there were districts in London like St George's-in-the-East, Golden Square, the east side of Regent Street, parts of Deptford, where it took even more life.[33] That very spring a Royal Commission on the Corporation of the City of London – the second in Victoria's reign – had proposed the establishment of a board of management for London beyond the ancient square mile, which would do for it what the Corporation had disdained to do and the 78 assorted vestries and 300 or so other bodies that held disputed sway over it could never do – cleanse it, improve it, govern it.[34] And with the creation of the Metropolitan Board of Works for that purpose within the next 12 months came the need for more systematized knowledge about the mechanisms of the metropolis.

We see from this time therefore a new era of more searching and analytical mapping of London than *Collins' Illustrated Atlas* could provide. That was a job for a man who was only then seriously setting up as a mapmaker – Edward Stanford. He had acquired most of Collins's plates at the end of the fifties and his six-inch *Library Map of London*, published in 1862, was the first thoroughgoing survey of London for nearly 40 years: it became the authentic basis for projecting the

M.B.W.'s plans. The ultimate development of cartography of that order is the *Atlas of London and the London Region* prepared under the direction of Emrys Jones and D. J. Sinclair and published in 70 folio sheets in 1968. London is now so large and knowledge of it so liable to be fragmented that the chief need is to try to see the metropolitan city as a regional whole, and to map its social and economic elements within a context of town-planning.

The little *Atlas* which has been reprinted here belongs to a different age and met a different need. The urban landscape had not up to that time been treated by mapmakers any differently from the rural landscape. The problem of handling its compacted form was still seen largely as one of scale. The idea of urban life as a new kind of social order, as a symbiosis of many species, that had to be represented in special ways, had scarcely yet occurred to cartographers. Why not show churches, schools, and public buildings, suggested the *Builder* in 1856, on maps of their own: ". . . parts of another plan, differently shaded, might show the conditions of mortality, crime, or ignorance, or of property, or pauperism, and the latest census or enquiry . . ."[35] That suggestion was swiftly followed and within the next two or three decades London got specialized maps galore.

Yet, apart from an incomplete Post Office list of streets dated 1857, with maps of the ten postal districts designated the year before, and a plethora of pocket-sized maps – including more than one for the waistcoat[36] – no other true pocket street atlas of London seems to have been published before the turn of the century.[37] What this suggests perhaps is that, for the great bulk of ordinary Londoners, continuous access to the larger mass, those outer corridors beyond the daily round, was not – as it must already have been for errand-boys, cab and delivery van drivers, and policemen – an urgent social or economic

necessity. What it certainly does mean is that *Collins' Illustrated Atlas of London* remains in a class of its own, the prototype of that now indispensable thing, a pocket atlas, not of the 7,000 streets of London in 1854 but of the 27,000 streets of London today.

H.J. Dyos
Christmas 1972

NOTES

1 'The greatness of London', *Working Man's Friend*, new series, I (1852), 59.

2 'The map of London a hundred years ago', *Gentleman's Magazine*, new series, XLII (1854), 17.

3 [George Dodd], 'Growth of the map of London', *Edinburgh Review*, CIV (1856), 52.

4 [G.A.Sala], 'The great invasion', *Household Words*, V (1852), 70.

5 Ralph Waldo Emerson, *English Traits*, ed. Howard Mumford Jones (Cambridge, Mass., 1966), 59.

6 See my paper 'Greater and greater London: notes on metropolis and provinces in the nineteenth and twentieth centuries' in *Britain and the Netherlands*, ed. J.S.Bromley and E.H.Kossmann (The Hague, 1971), 89–112.

7 'The Nation of London', being ch. 7 of his *Autobiographic Sketches 1790–1803* (1862), 179. I owe this reference to my colleague, Philip Collins.

8 See, for example, John Hogg, *London As It Is* (1837); Paul Pry [*pseud*. Thomas Hill], *Oddities of London Life* (2 vols, 1838); [James Grant], *Travels in Town* (2 vols, 1839) and *Lights and Shadows of London Life* (2 vols, 1842).

9 Andrew Wynter, 'Country houses for the working classes', *People's Journal*, II (1846), 134.

10 G.A.S[ala], 'Fishers of men: or recruiting for Her Majesty's Forces in London', *Illustrated Times*, V (1857), 379.

11 J.F.Murray, *The World of London* (1844), I, 20–1.

12 See J.B.Harley, *Maps for the Local Historian* (1972), 7–15.

13 See Ida Darlington and James Howgego, *Printed Maps of London circa 1553–1850* (1964), an invaluable source of information from which much of my information about earlier maps has been derived.

14 The whole work, edited by Charles Welch, was published in facsimile by the London & Middlesex Archaeological Society in 1895.

15 A facsimile edition of this plan was published for the London Topographical Society in 1913–19, and a new reproduction, including the Index, has recently been issued by Harry Margary and Phillimore & Company.

16 Ralph Hyde, 'Printed Maps of London: 1851–1900' (unpublished F.L.A. thesis, 1971), 2. I am most grateful to the author, not only for giving me access to his sterling work but for commenting most helpfully on the draft of this Introduction.

17 See R.A.Skelton, 'The Ordnance Survey 1791–1825', *British Museum Quarterly,* XXI (1957–9), 59–61, and Ida Darlington, 'Edwin Chadwick and the first large-scale Ordnance Survey of London', *Transactions of the London & Middlesex Archaeological Society,* XXII (1969), 58–63; J.B.Harley and C.W.Phillips, *The Historian's Guide to Ordnance Survey Maps* (1964).

18 See Philippa Glanville's luxurious anthology, *London in Maps* (1972), especially p. 39.

19 *Tallis's London Street Views* had originally been issued in 88 parts in 1838–40, and these were reprinted by Nattali & Maurice in association with the London Topographical Society in 1969, along with the 1847 edition and a most useful introduction and biographical note by Peter Jackson.

20 Peter Cunningham, *Hand-Book of London* (enlarged edn, 1850), xxxiii.

21 (a) *London at a Glance. An Illustrated Atlas of London* appeared in September 1859 little different from the 1854 edition except for the addition of a list of about 250 hotels, the new postal districts, and the railways; the original publisher's and engraver's names were cut out. (b) *London at a Glance. A Guide for Visitors to the International Exhibition* appeared in 1862 identical in all respects to the 1859 edition except for the addition of more railways and a separate postal district map: it was, however, worse printed on inferior paper and filled out by advertisements.

22 [Cyrus Redding], 'London from the crow's nest', *Fraser's Magazine,* XXXIX (1849), 63.

23 On this episode, see my two-part paper, 'Railways and housing in Victorian London', *Journal of Transport History,* II (1955), 11–21, 90–100.

24 See J.E.Bradfield, *Notes on Toll Reform and the Turnpike and Ticket System* (1856).

25 'The toll-bar nuisance', *Illustrated London News*, xxx (1857), 535–6; for a map of London tollgates see pp. 554–5.

26 'The wants of London', *Illustrated London News*, xxv (1854), 294.

27 'Our Mean Metropolis', *Punch*, xxvii (1854), 158. See my 'Note on the objects of street improvement in Regency and early Victorian London', *International Review of Social History*, ii (1957), 259–65, and Anthony Sutcliffe, *The Autumn of Central Paris* (1970), ch. 2.

28 *Illustrated London News*, xxv (1854), 293; for more complaint about the inadequacies of the streets, see *ibid.*, xxiv (1854), 18, 24.

29 For a side-light on the social significance of street names see [E.Fairfax Taylor], 'London topography and street-nomenclature', *Edinburgh Review*, cxxxi (1870), 155–93.

30 Based on an estimate formed by evidence supplied to the Select Committee on Metropolitan Communications, 1854–5: T.C.Barker and Michael Robbins, *A History of London Transport*, Vol. I: *The Nineteenth Century* (1963), ch. 2.

31 [Andrew Wynter], 'The London commissariat', *Quarterly Review*, xcv (1854), 284, 292, 305.

32 Cyrus Redding, *op. cit.*, 60.

33 *Annual Register*, Chronicle for 1854, pp. 159–60; *Illustrated London News*, xxv (1854), 230.

34 On the state of the public administration of London at this time, see Sir Benjamin Hall's introductory speech on the Metropolis Local Management Bill in March 1855: *Hansard*, 3rd Series, cxxxvii, 699–722; it was reprinted at some length in G.Laurence Gomme, *London in the Reign of Victoria (1837–1897)* (1898), 42–56.

35 Quoted by Hyde, *op. cit.*, 44.

36 J.Skinner, *Waistcoat Pocket Map of London* [*c.* 1876]; *Letts's Waistcoat Pocket Map of London* [*c.* 1884], which was in fact an updated version of B.R.Davies's map of 1843, originally published for the Society for the Diffusion of Useful Knowledge, and now given a new format; there was another edition in 1887.

37 Bacon's *Up to Date Pocket Atlas and Guide to London* (1894) seems to have been the first that did not need a poacher's pocket to hold it; another was Philip's *A.B.C. Pocket Atlas-Guide to London* [1902]. Those described as 'portable' or 'handy' were generally about six inches by nine.

BIBLIOGRAPHICAL NOTE

Collins' Illustrated Atlas of London was first published in London by H. G. Collins in 1854. Two subsequent editions, incorporating minor additions, were published in London under different titles. In 1859 Thomas Hodgson published a new edition entitled *London at a Glance; An Illustrated Atlas of London*. In 1862 Darton & Hodge published a further edition as *London at a Glance: A Guide for Visitors to the International Exhibition*.

The present volume reprints photographically the first edition of 1854.

COLLINS'

Illustrated

ATLAS

OF

LONDON,

WITH 7000 REFERENCES,

In 36 Plates of the Principal Routes between

ST. PAUL'S AND THE SUBURBS,

From

A SURVEY

MADE EXPRESSLY FOR THIS WORK

BY R. JARMAN ESQ.

LONDON,

PUBLISHED BY H.G. COLLINS, 22, PATERNOSTER ROW.

Ent.ᵈ at .Stationers'Hall.

CONTENTS.

1. INTRODUCTION.

2. LIST OF PLATES.

3. LIST OF ILLUSTRATIONS.

4. GENERAL INDEX OF ROUTES.

5. INDEX TO THE STREETS.

6. LIST OF PUBLIC BUILDINGS, &c.

7. LIST OF EXHIBITIONS, &c.

8. KEY MAP.

9. THE THIRTY-SIX PLATES.

INTRODUCTION.

If the reader has ever seen an unfortunate stranger in one of our busy thoroughfares examining, almost hopelessly, the square yard of paper, with its complicated network of streets and houses, which (if we except the "River Thames," lying like a large eel on its surface,) is the principal idea to be gathered at the moment from the "Map of London" before him,—if the reader has ever seen this, he will be quite ready to acknowledge that some more convenient guide is necessary for use in the streets.

The simple fact is, that our Metropolis has grown to so enormous an extent—covering a surface of at least fifty square miles—that to take in the whole at one view, for any purpose of reference to a particular locality, is a proceeding productive of little more than useless annoyance and bewilderment.

We can gather from a Map of Europe a good general idea of the situation and extent of the particular countries included thereon, but only a very vague one of these in detail. We take another map of a part—say England and Wales—and we obtain a tolerably clear notion of the size and position of each county; but, if we desire more exact information, we take the map of one of these counties, and are thus assisted to the particular knowledge in view.

So we take a Map of London: unless it be of very large size, it is either a mass of confusion, which requires time and study to unravel, or merely gives the principal thoroughfares; as a Map of Europe shows only the more prominent features thereof, leaving you to consult your Atlas for minor details. It so happens that, in the case of the Metropolis, these 'minor details' are the very things requisite; for, if you wish to find one of the many streets between Oxford Street and Piccadilly, or between Hampstead Road and Regent's Park, any map which shows only the larger thoroughfares will be very inefficient; and a complete one, from its large size, will be so inconvenient as to be nearly useless for street use. As but very few of the residents in London are well acquainted with districts beyond their own localities, and still fewer have an intimate knowledge of its whole extent; it is clear that the Londoner, when seeking any particular point of his own city, is continually compelled, like the stranger, to have recourse to his Sheet Map; and, like him, to make up for its deficiencies by a number of troublesome inquiries.

The present work has been constructed for the purpose, if possible, of obviating all difficulties connected with the subject. The Metropolis has been divided into districts, each of which includes some principal route, or portion thereof, from one well-known point to another; these are engraved on thirty-six plates, and a small Map of the whole is attached, where the chief thoroughfares are clearly delineated. The stranger in London has only to consult the latter, to find his way from any one part of the town to another; and the copious Index will at once show him in which particular Map, and on what part thereof, to seek for the Square or Street he may be in search of. The size of the work admits of its being consulted in the streets, without notice or inconvenience of any kind.

As the terrestrial Atlas, with its detailed information, has been found a useful assistant to the geographical student, so, it is respectfully submitted, will THE ATLAS OF LONDON prove to be a valuable guide, both to the inhabitants of the Metropolis and its occasional visitants.

LONDON, *June* 1, 1854.

LIST OF PLATES.

PLATE 1. St. Paul's to Trafalgar Square, Westminster Abbey; Southwark, Blackfriars, Waterloo, Hungerford, and Westminster Bridges.

" 2. Trafalgar Square to the Parks and Belgrave Square.

" 3. Hyde Park to Kensington and Brompton.

" 4. St. James' Park to Mill Bank, Vauxhall Bridge, and Pimlico.

" 5. St. James' Park to Chelsea, Fulham Road, and Battersea Bridge.

" 6. St. Paul's to Oxford Street and Tottenham Court Road.

" 7. Oxford Street to New Road, Hyde Park, and Edgeware Road.

" 8. Edgeware Road to Great Western Railway Terminus and Kilburn Gate.

" 9. Oxford Street to Great Western Railway Terminus and Bayswater.

" 10. St. Paul's to Great Northern Railway Terminus, King's Cross, and Angel Inn, Islington.

" 11. King's Cross to North-Western Railway Terminus and Regent's Park.

" 12. Regent's Park to Kilburn Gate.

" 13. King's Cross to Regent's Park and Haverstock Hill.

" 14. King's Cross to Camden Road and Holloway.

" 15. St. Paul's (and Bank) to Hoxton, New North Road, and Angel Inn, Islington.

" 16. Angel Inn, Islington, to Holloway and Highbury.

" 17. Angel Inn, Islington, to Ball's Pond Road and Kingsland Road.

" 18. St. Paul's (and Bank) to Eastern Counties Railway Terminus, Shoreditch, and Kingsland Road.

" 19. Kingsland Road to Dalston, Shacklewell, Hackney, and Stoke Newington Road.

" 20. Shoreditch to Hackney Road, Bethnal Green, and Victoria Park.

" 21. Hackney Road to Victoria Park, Hackney, Homerton, and Clapton.

" 22. St. Paul's to London Bridge, Blackwall Railway Terminus, London Docks, and Whitechapel
Church.

" 23. Whitechapel Church to Limehouse Church and Bow Road.

" 24. Bow Road to Old Ford, Victoria Park, Hackney, and Homerton.

" 25. London Docks to Thames Tunnel and Limehouse Church.

" 26. Limehouse Church to Poplar, West India Docks, and Isle of Dogs.

" 27. The Six Bridges to South-Western and London Bridge Railway Termini, Borough Road, and
Elephant and Castle Inn.

" 28. London Bridge to Bermondsey and Thames Tunnel.

" 29. Thames Tunnel to Deptford, by Rotherhithe and the River Side.

" 30. Thames Tunnel to Deptford, by the Lower Road.

" 31. Elephant and Castle Inn to Bermondsey, Bricklayers' Arms Railway Station, and Old Kent
Road.

" 32. Old Kent Road to New Cross.

" 33. Borough Road and Elephant and Castle Inn to Surrey Gardens, Kennington Common, and
Camberwell.

" 34. Surrey Gardens to Walworth and Old Kent Road.

" 35. Westminster Bridge to Clapham Road, and Nine Elms, Vauxhall.

" 36. Nine Elms to Battersea Bridge.

5

LIST OF ILLUSTRATIONS.

———

Bank of England .... Plate 18

British Museum.. 6

Buckingham Palace 5

Christ Church, Battersea Fields 36

Elephant and Castle Inn 31

General Post-Office.. 10

Great Northern Railway Terminus... 13

Guildhall.. 18

Islington Church.. 16

Limehouse Church 26

London Bridge.. 28

Marble Arch, Hyde Park 7

Model Prison, Pentonville 14

Nelson Column 2

Newgate Prison 10

Rotherhithe, from Wapping... 25

Royal Exchange 18

Sadler's Wells Theatre 15

St. George's Church, Camberwell 34

St. Mark's Church, Kennington Common.. 33

St. Mary's Hospital 8

St. Paul's Cathedral 1

St. Paul's Church, Ball's Pond... 17

St. Philip's Church, Dalston... 19

St. Saviour's Church, Southwark 27

Shoreditch Church 20

Sussex Place, Regent's Park 11

Thames Tunnel 29

The Holme, Regent's Park 12

Tower of London.. 22

Trinity Church, Bishop's Road 9

Victoria Park 20

Walworth Lecture Hall... 34

Westminster Abbey... 4

GENERAL INDEX OF ROUTES.

NORTH OF THE THAMES.

ST. PAUL'S,

    Westward to

THE RIVER THAMES,
WESTMINSTER,
KENSINGTON,
BROMPTON,
MILL BANK,
PIMLICO,
VAUXHALL,
BATTERSEA,
FULHAM ROAD.

St. Paul's to Blackfriars Bridge .... Plate 1
St. Paul's to Waterloo Bridge 1
St. Paul's to Hungerford Bridge 1
St. Paul's to Westminster Bridge.. 1
St. Paul's to Trafalgar Square 1
Trafalgar Square to the Parks 2
Trafalgar Square to Belgrave Square 2
Hyde Park Corner to Brompton 3
Hyde Park Corner to Kensington 3
St. James' Park to Mill Bank... 4
St. James' Park to Pimlico.. 4
St. James' Park to Vauxhall Bridge... 4
St. James' Park to Chelsea 5
St. James' Park to Battersea Bridge... 5
St. James' Park to Fulham Road 5

ST. PAUL'S,

    Westward to

OXFORD STREET,
PADDINGTON,
KILBURN,
BAYSWATER.

St. Paul's to Oxford Street.. Plate 6
St. Paul's to Tottenham Court Road 6
Oxford Street to New Road 7
Oxford Street to Edgeware Road 7
Edgeware Road to Kilburn Gate 8
Oxford Street to Hyde Park and Kensington Gardens 9
Oxford Street to Bayswater... 9
Oxford Street to Great Western Railway Terminus......................... 9

ST. PAUL'S,

    Northward to

KING'S CROSS,
ISLINGTON,
REGENT'S PARK,
KILBURN,
CAMDEN TOWN,
KENTISH TOWN,
HAVERSTOCK HILL,
HOLLOWAY.

St. Paul's to Clerkenwell .... Plate 10
St. Paul's to Pentonville... 10
St. Paul's to King's Cross.. 10
St. Paul's to Angel Inn, Islington... 10
St. Paul's to Great Northern Railway Terminus 10
King's Cross to North-Western Railway Terminus........................... 11
King's Cross to Marylebone 11
King's Cross to Regent's Park 11
Regent's Park to Kilburn Gate 12
King's Cross to Camden Town 13
King's Cross to Kentish Town Road... 13
King's Cross to Haverstock Hill 13
King's Cross to Holloway... 14

ST. PAUL'S,

    Northward to

ISLINGTON,
HOLLOWAY,
HIGHBURY,
NEWINGTON GREEN,
KINGSLAND.

St. Paul's (and Bank) to Angel Inn, Islington........................... Plate 15
St. Paul's (and Bank) to Hoxton.. 15
St. Paul's (and Bank) to New North Road 15
Angel Inn, Islington, to Canonbury 16
Angel Inn, Islington, to Holloway... 16
Angel Inn, Islington, to Highbury 16
Angel Inn, Islington, to Newington Green 17
Angel Inn, Islington, to Kingsland Gate 17

ST. PAUL'S,

    Northward to

KINGSLAND ROAD,
STOKE NEWINGTON ROAD,
DALSTON,
SHACKLEWELL,
HACKNEY,
HOMERTON,
CLAPTON,
BETHNAL GREEN,
VICTORIA PARK.

St. Paul's (and Bank) to Shoreditch and Eastern Counties Railway
    Terminus .... Plate 18
St. Paul's (and Bank) to Kingsland Road 18
Kingsland Road to Dalston 19
Kingsland Road to Shacklewell 19
Kingland's Road to Stoke Newington Road 19
Kingsland Road to Hackney... 19
Shoreditch to Bethnal Green 20
Shoreditch to Cambridge Heath... 20
Shoreditch to Old Ford... 20
Shoreditch to Victoria Park... 20
Cambridge Heath to Hackney... 21
Cambridge Heath to Homerton... 21
Cambridge Heath to Clapton.. 21
Victoria Park to Clapton 21

NORTH OF THE THAMES.

(*Continued.*)

St. Paul's,

   Eastward to

   The River Thames,
   Whitechapel,
   Shadwell,
   Ratcliffe,
   Wapping,
   Limehouse,
   Poplar,
   Isle of Dogs,
   Bow Road,
   Victoria Park,
   Homerton.

St. Paul's to London Bridge .... Plate 22
St. Paul's to Blackwall Railway Terminus.. 22
St. Paul's to London Docks and St. George's East............................. 22
St. Paul's to Whitechapel Church 22
Whitechapel Church to Limehouse 23
Whitechapel Church to Bow Road... 23
Bow Road to Old Ford 24
Bow Road to Victoria Park ....\. 24
Bow Road to Hackney and Homerton 24
London Docks to Wapping and Thames Tunnel............................. 25
London Docks to Shadwell and Ratcliff 25
London Docks to Limehouse Church 25
Limehouse Church to Poplar and West India Docks...................... 26
Limehouse Church to Isle of Dogs 26

SOUTH OF THE THAMES.

The Six Bridges,

   Eastward to

   Borough Road and
   Elephant and Castle Inn,
   Bermondsey,
   Rotherhithe,
   Deptford.

The Six Bridges to London Bridge Railway Terminus............ Plate 27
The Six Bridges to Borough Road... 27
The Six Bridges to Elephant and Castle Inn 27
The Six Bridges to South-Western Railway Terminus 27
London Bridge to Bermondsey 28
London Bridge to Rotherhithe.. 28
London Bridge to Thames Tunnel 28
Thames Tunnel to Commercial Docks 29
Thames Tunnel to Deptford by the River Side 29
Thames Tunnel to Deptford by the Road 30

Elephant and Castle Inn,

   Eastward to

   Walworth,
   Bermondsey,
   Old Kent Road,
   New Cross.

Elephant and Castle to East Street, Walworth .... Plate 31
Elephant and Castle to Bermondsey 31
Elephant and Castle to Bricklayers' Arms Railway Terminus......... 31
Elephant and Castle to Old Kent Road.. 31
Old Kent Road to New Cross 32

Elephant and Castle Inn,

   Southward to

   Kennington Common,
   Walworth,
   Camberwell,
   Clapham Road,
   Brixton Road,
   Old Kent Road.

Elephant and Castle to Surrey Gardens .... Plate 33
Elephant and Castle to Walworth.. 33
Elephant and Castle to Camberwell 33
Elephant and Castle to Kennington Common 33
Elephant and Castle to Clapham Road.. 33
Elephant and Castle to Brixton Road 33
Surrey Gardens to Walworth 34
Surrey Gardens to Old Kent Road.. 43

Borough Road and
Westminster Bridge,

   Westward to

   Kennington Common,
   Clapham Road,
   Lambeth,
   Vauxhall,
   South Lambeth,
   Wandsworth Road,
   Nine Elms,
   Battersea.

Borough Road to Kennington Cross .... Plate 35
Borough Road to Lambeth 35
Borough Road to Vauxhall 35
Borough Road to South Lambeth 35
Borough Road to Wandsworth Road.. 35
Borough Road to Nine Elms 35
Westminster Bridge to Kennington Common 35
Westminster Bridge to Clapham Road 35
Westminster Bridge to Vauxhall 35
Westminster Bridge to South Lambeth 35
Westminster Bridge to Wandsworth Road.................................... 35
Westminster Bridge to Nine Elms... 35
Nine Elms to Battersea Bridge 36

INDEX TO THE STREETS.

Each Plate is numbered Plate 1, 2, 3, &c., and divided into four quarters, marked A, B, C, D. To these numbers and letters those in the Index refer.

EXAMPLE—"Abbey Place, Abbey Road, Plate 8, D; 12, C," which will be found in Plate 8, in the quarter marked D; and also on Plate 12, in the quarter marked C.

Abbey place, Abbey road ....Plate 8, D; 12, C
    ″   road.......................................12, C; 1, D
    ″   street, Bermondsey.....................28, B; 31, C
    ″   ″ Bethnal green road.......... 20, B; 23, A
Abchurch lane..22, B
Abdy street...28, A
Abercorn place, Edgeware road .... 8, D; 12. C
Aberdeen place, Maida hill ....8, B
Abingdon street, Bethnal green ....20, D
    ″   ″ Westminster ....4, A
Acacia road ....12, B
Acorn street ....18, B
Active place, Spa road ....28, D; 31, C
Acton street, Gray's Inn road ....10, C
    ″   ″ Kingsland road ....19, A
Ada street ....21, A
Adam's mews..2, D; 7, C
Adam street, Adelphi, Strand ....1, D; 27, D
    ″   ″ East......................................7, D
    ″   ″ New Kent road ....31, B
    ″   ″ Rotherhithe............. 28, D, 29, B; 30, A
    ″   ″ West......................7, D; 8, A; 9, A
Addington square, Camberwell road ....33, C; 34, B
    ″   street, do.   ....34, B
    ″   ″ York road, Westminster.....27, C
Addle hill ....1, B; 15, A
    ″ street ....15, B
Adelaide road ....13, D
    ″ street ....1, D
Ægis grove..36, A
Adelphi terrace ....1, D; 27, D
Agar street ....1, D
Air street ....2, B
Albany ....2, B
    ″ road, Barnsbury park ....14, D
    ″ ″ Camberwell .... 31, D; 33, C; 34, B C D
    ″ row, do. ....34, D
    ″ street, Albany road, Camberwell ....34, B
    ″ ″ Commercial road, East .... 23, D
    ″ ″ Regent's park ....11, C
    ″ ″ Little, do. ....11, C
    ″ ″ Upper, do. ....11, D; 13, C
Albemarle street...2, B
Albert gate ....3, A
Albert place, Ball's pond road ....20, C; 21, B
    ″ grove ....19, C
    ″ ″ Kensington ....3, D
    ″ road, Dalston ....21, A
    ″ ″ Globe fields ....24, A
    ″ ″ Regent's park ....12, B; 13, C
    ″ square, Clapham road ....35, C
    ″ ″ Commercial road, East .... 23, D; 25, C
    ″ street, Cambridge road.........................20, D
    ″ ″ Camden-town ....13, D
    ″ ″ Evelyn street, Deptford ..... 29, D; 30, C
    ″ ″ Great Cambridge street ....19, B
    ″ ″ Gt. George st., Bermondsey, 28, B; 31, C

Albert street, Mile-end, New-town ....Plate 23, A
    ″ ″ Mornington crescent .... 13, C
    ″ ″ Kennington road .... 33, D; 34, A
    ″ ″ Pentonville .... 14, B; 16, A
    ″ ″ Shadwell ....25, B
Albert terrace, Bayswater ....9, D
    ″ ″ London road ....35, A
    ″ ″ Pentonville.................... 14, B; 16, A
    ″ ″ Regent's park ....13, C
Albion grove ....14, B; 16, A
    ″ place, Blackfriars' bridge ....27, B
    ″ ″ Clerkenwell .... 15, A
    ″ ″ Walworth road................. 33, A; 34, A
    ″ road, Dalston ....19, B; 21, A
    ″ ″ Hackney .... 21, D
    ″ ″ Liverpool road .... 14, D; 16, C
    ″ square......................................19, A
    ″ street, Caledonian road...........13, B; 14, A
    ″ ″ Hyde park .... 7, D; 8, A; 9, A
    ″ ″ Mile-end................................23, C
    ″ ″ Rotherhithe .... 28, D; 29, B; 30, A
    ″ ″ Winchester street.....................23, A
Aldenham street ....13, B
Aldermanbury ....15, B; 18, A
Alderman's walk..22, A
Alderney place ....23, C
Aldersgate street .... 6, A; 15, A; 18, A
Aldgate, High street ....22, C
Aldred road ....33, D
Alexander square ....3, C
    ″ street ....32, B
Alfred place, Bedford square .... 6, D; 7, B
    ″ ″ Old Kent road .... 31, D; 34, C
    ″ ″ Thurloe square ....3, C
    ″ street, Bedford square ....6, D
    ″ ″ Bow road.................................24, B
    ″ ″ City road ....15, C; 17, A
    ″ ″ Ferry road, West ....26, D
    ″ ″ Grange road ....31, C
    ″ ″ Maiden lane, Battle bridge....... 14, C
    ″ ″ South Lambeth ....35, C
    ″ ″ Vincent square ....4, D
    ″ ″ Whitehorse lane ....23, C
Alice street ....31, A
Alie street, Great ....22, C
    ″ ″ Little ....22, C; 23, B
Allan street ....16, B; 17, A
Allen street, Goswell street ....15, C
    ″ ″ Westminster ....35, B
    ″ ″ York road, Old Kent road ...31, D; 34, C
Allerton street, Hoxton ....15, D; 18, C
Allington street ....4, B
All-hallows lane ....22, B
All-Saints' place, Caledonian road ....14, B
Allsops place, Regent's park .... 8, B; 11, C; 12, A
Allsop terrace, New road ....8, B
Almina place, Maiden lane, Battle bridge......... 14, C

Alpha place, Alpha road ....Plate 8, B
　" 　" 　Cambridge road .... 23, A
Alpha road...8, B ; 12, A
　" 　street, Chelsea......................................5, C
　" 　" 　Old Kent road....................32, B; 34, D
Alscot road........ ....31, C
Alwyne road..16, D; 17, C
Amelia place, Spa road...............................28, D; 31, C
　" 　street, Old Kent road............31, D ; 34 C
　" 　" 　Walworth road...............33, A ; 34, A
Amen corner ....15, A
America square .... 22, D
Amersham road...32, D
Amherst road ....19, D; 21, C
Ampthill square.......................................11, B ; 13, A
Ampton street...10, C
Amwell street ....10, D
Anchor street..18, D; 20, B
Anderson street .... 5, D
Andrew's road..20, C ; 21, A
Angel street...............................6, A ; 10, B ; 15, A
Ann street, Coburg road.................................34, D
　" 　" 　Green street, Bethnal green............20, D
　" 　" 　Kent street ....31, A
　" 　" 　Pentonville ....10, C ; 14, B
　" 　" 　St. George's, East..........................25, A
　" 　" 　St. Paul's square........................17, A
　" 　" 　Thurlow place, Walworth....31, A ; 34, A
　" 　" 　Trafalgar 　 do. 　 ....31, B
　" 　" 　Wilmot square................................20, B
Ann's place, Kent street...........................28, B; 31, A
　" 　row, Thurlow place, Walworth....31, B; 34, A
　" 　terrace, Coburg road.............................34, D
Annette's crescent..17,⁴C
Anthony street..22, C ; 25, A
Arabella row, Pimlico.............................2, C; 5, B
Arbour place, Arbour square ....23, D
　" 　square..23, D
　" 　street, East..............................23, D; 25, C
　" 　" 　West ....23, D; 25, C
Archer street, Camden-town.........................13, D
　" 　" 　Great Windmill street.........2, B; 6, C
　" 　" 　South Lambeth.........................35, D
Appleby street ....19, B
Argyle square..10, C; 11, B
　" 　street...10, C; 11, B; 13, A
Argyll place, Regent street..............................7, A
　" 　street ....7, A
Arlington square..17, B
　" 　street, Camden-town...............:.........13, C
　" 　" 　New North road.....................17, B
　" 　" 　Piccadilly..............................2, B
　" 　" 　St. John street road..............10, D
Arnold's paragon...................................33, A ; 34, A
Arthur street, Chelsea......................................5, C
　" 　" 　Great, Golden lane..................15, A
　" 　" 　Gray's Inn road.......................10, C
　" 　" 　London bridge........... ....22, B
　" 　" 　Old Kent road........................32, B
　" 　" 　Oxford street.............................6, C
　" 　" 　Well street, Hackney ......21, D; 24, C
Artichoke hill...25, A
Artillery court ....15, B
　" 　lane, Bishopsgate.............................22, A
　" 　" 　Horselydown........................28, A
　" 　place, Finsbury ....15, B; 18 C
　" 　row, Westminster...............................4, B
　" 　street, Bethnal green..........................23, A
　" 　" 　Bishopsgate....................18, B
　" 　" 　Horselydown.......................28, A
Arundel road...19, C
　" 　square..14, D; 16, C
　" 　street, Kingsland.............................19, C
　" 　" 　Strand..........................1, B; 6, A
　" 　" 　Waterloo town ....20, B; 23, A
Ash grove ....20, C; 21, A
Ashby street, King's cross............................13, B
　" 　" 　Northampton square..................15, C
Ashford street..18, C

Ashley crescent ....Plate 15, D; 17, B
　" 　place, Westminster....................... 4, B; 5, B
Aske street...18, C
Aston street..23, D ; 25, C
Asylum road...32, B
Augustus square..................................11, D; 13, A
　" 　street, East India Dock road ....26, A
　" 　" 　Regent's park.............11, D; 13, A
Austin Friars...18, B
　" 　street...18, D
Avebury street..17, B
Ave Maria lane...........................1, B; 6, A; 10, B
Avenue road...12, B
Avery row...7, A
Aylesbury street, Clerkenwell........................15, C
　" 　" 　Walworth.......................34, C
Ayliffe street..31, B

Baalzephon street..............................28, B; 31, A
Bacchus walk...18, C; 19, A
Back hill...10, A
　" 　road , Kingsland.................................19, C
　" 　street...28, A
　" 　way, Pancras road...........................13, B
Back Church lane........................22, C; 23, B; 25, A
Bacon street ....18, D; 20, B
Bagnigge Wells road..10, C
Bainbridge street...6, C
Baker street, Bedford square, East.........23, B; 25, C
　" 　" 　Green st., Bethnal green.....20, D; 24, A
　" 　" 　Lloyd square............................10, C
　" 　" 　Upper 　 do. 　........................10, C
　" 　" 　Portman square...........................7, D
　" 　" 　Upper 　 do. 　.......8, B; 11, C; 12, A
　" 　" 　Walworth road............................33, A
Baker's row, Clerkenwell.................................10, C
　" 　" 　Whitechapel road......................23, A
Baldwin street ....15, D; 18, C
Baldwin's gardens................................6, B; 10, A
Ball's pond road ....17, C D; 19, C
Baltic place, Deptford, Lower road...................30, A
　" 　street ....15, A
Bancroft place ....23, C ; 24, A
Bankside..1, A; 27, B
Banner street..15, D
Barbican..15, A
Barclay street...13, A
Barford street...16, A
Bark place...9, C
Barlow street, Great..7, D
Barnard's Inn...6, A; 10, A
Barnes street..23, D; 25, C
Barnett's grove..20, A
Barnham street..28, A
Barnsbury grove ....14, D
　" 　park..14, D ; 16, C
　" 　road.....................................14, B; 16, A
　" 　square...................................14, D; 16, A
　" 　street...16, A
　" 　" 　Upper.......................................14, D; 16, A
Barnsley street...23, A
Baron street...10, D; 14, B; 16, A
Baron's place, Waterloo road...........................27, C
Barrett grove...19, C
　" 　street...35, C
Barrowhill road...12, A
Bartholomew close....................6, A; 10, B; 15, A
　" 　lane...........................18, A; 22, B
　" 　place,Trap street, Bethnal green....23, A
　" 　square..15, D
Bartlett's buildings.................................6, A; 10, A
Basing place, Kingsland road ....18, C; 20, A
Basinghall street....................................15, B; 18, A
Bateman's row, Shoreditch.................18, D; 20, B
Bath place, York road, Battle bridge....13, B; 14, A
　" 　" 　Surrey canal..................................34, B
　" 　road ....32, B
　" 　row, Dalston ....19, C
　" 　street, Bird Cage walk............................20, A

Bath street, Cambridge road..................Plate 20, D
„ „ City road..................... 15, D
„ „ London road .... 33, B
„ „ Newgate street..............1, B; 15, A
„ „ Albany road, Camberwell..............34, B
„ „ Tabernacle square.......................18, C
„ „ Great, Clerkenwell ....10, C
„ terrace, Horsemonger lane ....31, A
Bathurst street.....................................9, A
Batson street...25, D
Battersea bridge..............................5, C; 36, D
„ „ road.............................36, C D
„ park (intended)............36, C D
„ road ....36, A C
Battle bridge...14, A
Batty street.............................22, C; 23, B
Bay street....................................19, A
Bayham place, Camden-town ....13, B
„ street................................13, D
Bayswater terrace.....................................9, C
Beak street..................................2, B; 7, A
Bear alley.....................................1, B; 10, A
„ garden.................................1, A; 27, B
„ lane..27, B
Bearbinder lane.......................................24, B
Beaufort buildings....................................1, D
„ street....................................5, C
Beaumont square.......................................23, C
„ street, Beaumont square.............23, C
„ „ Portland place...............7, B; 11, C
Bedford place, Russell square........................6, D
„ „ Upper, do. ....6, D; 11, A
„ row, Holborn.....................6, D; 10, A
„ „ Southwark.......................27, B
„ square ....6, D; 7, A
„ „ East............................23, B
„ street, Ampthill square...............11, B
„ „ Bedford square.............6, D; 7, A
„ „ Commercial road, East....23, B; 25, A
„ „ Holborn ....6, D; 10, A
„ „ Strand...........................1, D
„ „ Walworth ....31, B; 33, A; 34, A
Bedfordbury,..1, D
Beech street, Barbican...............................15, B
„ „ South Lambeth new road .... 35, C
Beer lane .... 22, D
Belgrave mews, East ....2, C; 3, A
„ place, Walworth .... 33, C; 34, A
„ road, Pimlico ....4, D; 5, A
„ square .... 2, C; 3, A; 5, B
„ street, Belgrave square................. 5, B
„ „ South, do......................... 5, B
„ „ Upper, do............. 2, C: 3, A; 5, B
„ „ Commercial road, East...23, D; 25, C
„ „ King's cross.......10, C; 11, B ; 13 A
„ terrace, Maismore square.........32, B; 34, D
Belinda terrace, New North road.......... 16, B; 17, C
Belitha villas .... 14, D
Bell alley, Great ....15, B; 18, A
„ „ Little ....,......... 15, B; 18, A
„ lane ....18, B; 22, A
„ street .... 8, A
„ yard, Temple-bar ....1, B; 6, A
Bell Wharf hill................................ 25, D
Belleveu. Chelsea....................................5, C
„ place, Mile-end............................. 23, A
Belvedere buildings....................................27, A
„ place, Borough road... 27, A; 31, A; 33, B
„ road .... 1, C; 27, C D; 35, B
Bemmerton street ....14, B
Benjamin street ....10, B; 15, A
Bennetts' buildings, Kennington lane......33, B; 35, A
Bennett's hill, ...1, A
Bennett street, Blackfriars' road .... 27, B
„ „ St. James'.......................... 2, B
Bentinck street, Vincent square .... 4, D
„ „ Manchester square ....7, B
Bentley's terrace, Kingsland road .... 17, D
Bere street .... 25, D

Beresford street ....Plate 33, C ; 34, B
Berkeley place, Connaught square .... 9, A
„ square .... 2, D
„ street, Clerkenwell .... 10, B; 15, A
„ „ Lambeth .... 35, B
„ „ Piccadilly .... 2, D
„ „ Portman square .... 7, D
„ „ Upper, Portman sq....7, D; 8, A ; 9, B
„ „ „ West ....7, D; 8, A ; 9, A
Bermondsey New road........................ 28, B; 31, A
„ square .... 28, B; 31, C
„ street....................28, A B; 31, A
„ wall .... 28, C D
Bernard street...............................6, D; 11, A
Berner street, Commercial rd., East...22, C; 23, B; 25, A
Berners street, Oxford street ....7, A
Berwick street, Belgrave road ....4, D
„ „ Oxford street.........................7, A
Besborough grove, Vauxhall bridge road .... 4, C
„ place, do. do. .... 4, C
„ road, do. do. .... 4, C
Bethnal green ....20, D
„ „ road................................ 20, B D
„ „ „ old..............................20, B D
Betts street................................ 22, C; 25, A
Bevenden street......................... 15, D; 18, C
Bevis Marks................................... 22, A
Bexley street.................................... 34, D
Bidborough street................................. 11, B
Billiter square .... 22, B
„ street...................................22, B
Bingfield street................................... 14, B
Birchin lane .... 18, B; 22, B
Bird street, Oxford street........................ 7, C
„ „ Lambeth.................... 33, B; 35, A
„ „ Wapping..........................25, B
Bird Cage walk, Bethnal green .... 20, A
„ „ „ St. James' park.............. 2, A; 4, B
Bishop's road, Bayswater...................... 8, A; 9, D
„ „ Victoria park .... 20, C; 21, B
„ walk............................. 35, B
Bishopsgate street .... 18, B; 22, A
Blackfriars bridge ....1, A; 27, B
„ „ road .... 27, A B; 33, B; 35, A
Black Horse fields ....30, C
Blackman street ....27, A; 31, A
Blackmoor street.................................1, D; 6, C
Bland street....................................... 31, A
„ „ Upper.................................. 31, A
„ „ Lower................................. 31, A
Blandford square .... 8, B
„ street ....7, D
Blenheim place, Oxford street.................... 7, A
„ road .... 12, D
„ street ....5, D
„ terrace, Abbey road.................... 12, C
Blomfield street, Finsbury .... 18, B
Bloomberg street ....4, C
Bloomfield gardens .... 8, C
„ place, Grosvenor row....................5, A
„ road ....8, C
„ street, Dalston .... 17, D; 19, A
Bloomsbury square ....6, D
„ street ....6, C
Blossom street .... 18, D
Blue Anchor lane .... 28, D; 30, B; 31, C
„ „ road.................. 28, D; 30, B; 31, C
„ „ yard.................... 22, D; 25, A
Bolton row, Piccadilly................................2, D
„ street, Kennington common .... 33, D
„ „ Piccadilly .... 2, D
Bolwell street .... 35, B
Bond street, New ....2, B; 7, A
„ „ Old .... 2, B
„ „ Borough road........................ 33, B
„ „ Chelsea..............................5, D
„ „ Lambeth............................27, D
„ „ Pentonville .... 10, D
„ „ Vauxhall ....35, D

Bonner road..Plate 20, C
    //   street..............................20, D; 24, A
Bonner's fields.......................20, C; 21, B; 24, A
Boot street...18, C
Booth street..23, A
Borough High street......................27, A B; 31, A
    //   Market...........................27, B; 28, A
    //   road ....27, A; 33, B, 35, A
Bostock street..25, B
Boston place, Boston street, Regent's park.........8, B
    //   street, Hackney road ....20, A
    //   //   Regent's park ....8, B; 12, A
Botolph lane..22, B
Boundary lane ....33, C; 34, B
    //   road ....12, D
    //   street...........................18, D; 20, B
Bourdon street ....2, D; 7, A
Bouverie street, Edgeware road ....8, A ; 9, B
    //   //   Fleet street.................1, B; 6, A
Bow common ....23, C
    //   //   lane ....23, C
    //   lane ....15, A; 18, A; 22, B
    //   road ....23, C; 24, B
    //   street ....6, C
Bower street ....23, D; 25, C
Bowling street ....4, A
    //   Green lane ....10, D
    //   //   street ....33, D; 35, C
    //   //   walk ....18, C
Boxworth grove ....14, B
Boytons place, Addington square...................34, B
Brackley street ....15, A
Brad street ....27, D
Bradley place, Wandsworth road ....35, D; 36, A
Bradshaw street..32, A
Braemer street ....24, A
Branch place, Hoxton...................................17, B
Brandon row, Newington causeway ......31, A; 33, B
    //   street, Bermondsey ....31, A
    //   //   Walworth...31, B; 33, A; 34, A
Bread street ....15, A; 18, A; 22, B
    //   hill ....1, A; 22, B
Bream's buildings, Chancery lane.....................6, A
Brecknock crescent ....13, C
    //   street ....13, D
Breezers hill..25, A
Brewer street, Goswell road ....10, D; 15, C
    //   //   Somers-town ....11, B; 13, A
    //   //   Pimlico ....4 B; 5 B
Brewhouse lane ....25, B
Brick lane, Old street...................................15, C
    //   //   Spitalfields ....18, D; 20, B; 23, A
    //   street ....2, D
    //   Hill lane ....22, B
Bride lane ....1, B; 6, A
    //   street ....14, D
    //   //   Great ....14, D; 16, C
Bridge place, Surrey canal...........................30, C
    //   road, Haverstock hill............................13, C
    //   //   Limehouse ....26, B
    //   //   Pimlico ....5, A
    //   //   St. John's wood ....12, D
    //   //   Westminster ....27, C; 35, B
    //   //   West, Battersea ....36, D
    //   street, Bermondsey ....28, B
    //   //   New, Blackfriars......1, B; 6, A; 10, A
    //   //   Little,   do.   ....1, B; 15, A
    //   //   Homerton ....21, D
    //   //   Mile-end,.................................23, C
    //   //   East do. ....23, C
    //   //   Southwark ....1, A; 27, B
    //   //   Westminster, 1, C; 4, A; 27, C; 35, B
Bridgewater square ....15, A
    //   street ....11, B; 13, A
Bridle lane ....7, A
Bridport place, New North road.............15, D; 17, B
Brighton street...11, B
Brill row, Somers-town.........................11, B; 13, A
  //   terrace,   do.   ....11, B; 13, A

Bristow street, Blackfriars ....Plate 1, B
    //   //   New North road ....17, B
Britannia place, Surrey canal...........................32, A
    //   street, City road ....15, D
    //   //   Gray's Inn road ....10, C
    //   //   Islington ....16, B; 17, A
Britten street ....5, C
Brixton road ....33, D; 35, C
Broad street, Golden square ....7, A
    //   //   Horselydown ....28, A
    //   //   Lambeth ....35, B
    //   //   New...18, B
    //   //   Old.............................18, B; 22, A
    //   //   Ratcliffe...................................25, D
    //   //   St. Giles' ....6, C
    //   //   Wapping ....25, B
    //   //   Buildings ....18, B
Broadley street, Blandford square......................8, B
    //   terrace,   do.   ....8, B
Broadwall ....27, D
Broadway, Ludgate hill ....1, B
    //   St. Thomas' hospital ....28, A
    //   Westminster ....4, A
Broke road ....19, B; 21, A
Broken wharf...1, A
Bromley street..............................23, D; 25, C
Brompton crescent ....3, C
    //   road ....3, A
    //   square ....3, C
Bronti street ....33, C; 34, A
Brook market ....10, A
    //   mews ....7, A
    //   place, Old Kent road ....31, D
    //   street, Bermondsey ....28, B; 31, A
    //   //   Grosvenor square ....7, C
    //   //   Upper,   do.   ......3, B; 7, C; 9, A
    //   //   Holborn ....6, B; 10, A
    //   //   Lambeth ....33, B; 35, A
    //   //   New road ....11, A
    //   //   Little, do. ....11, C
    //   //   Ratcliffe ....25, D
Brooksby street..............................14, D; 16, A
Brown street, Oxford street..............................7, C
    //   //   Seymour place ....8, A
Brownlow road ....19, B; 21, A
    //   street, Dalston..................................19, B
    //   //   Drury lane ....6, C
    //   //   Holborn ....6, D; 10, A
Brown's lane..18, D
    //   place, Shacklewell ....19, C
Brunswick court, Horselydown........................28, A
    //   place, City road ....18, C
    //   //   Regent's park ....11, C
    //   road ....33, C
    //   square.....................................11, A
    //   street, Back Church lane.................25, A
    //   //   Barnsbury road ....14, B
    //   //   Great Dover street ....31, A
    //   //   Hackney road ....19, B; 20, A
    //   //   Stamford street ....27, D
    //   //   Well street, Hackney, 21, D; 24, C
    //   terrace, Park road, Old Kent road... 32, B
    //   //   Camberwell road .....33, C; 34, B
Brunton's place, Commercial road, East..23, D; 25, D
Bruton place, Berkeley square..................2, D; 7, A
    //   street,   do.   ....2, B; 7, A
Bryan place, Caledonian road........................14, B
    //   street,   do.   ....14, B
Bryanstone square ....7, D; 8, A
    //   street ....7, C
    //   //   Upper ....7, C; 9, A
Brydges street ....1, D; 6 C
Buck street ....13, D
Buckingham cottages ....4, D
    //   road ....17, D
    //   row, Westminster ....4, B
    //   street, Caledonian road................14, D
    //   //   Fitzroy square ....7, B
    //   //   Strand ....1, D; 27, D

Buckingham street, William street, Caledonian road ....Plate 14, B
Buckle street..22. C
Bucklersbury.......................................18. A; 22, B
Budge row ....15, B; 18, A; 22, B
Bull lane ....23, C
Bull and Mouth street ....6, A; 10, B
Bulstrode street ....7, B
Burdett street, Walworth ....34, A
    //   //   Westminster road ....27, C; 35, A
Burlington arcade ....2, B
    //   gardens ....2, B
    //   street..2, B
    //   //   New ....7, A
Burnard terrace, Eden grove ....14, D
Burne street ....8, A
Buross street ....23, B; 25, A
Burr street...22, D
Burton crescent ....11, B
    //   street, do....................................11, B
    //   //   Cambridge road......................23, A
    //   //   Pimlico ....5, B
    //   //   Walworth................................34, A
Bury street, Bloomsbury..................................6, D
    //   //   Fulham road ....5, D
    //   //   St. James' ....2, B
    //   //   St. Mary Axe ....22, A
Busby street ....20, B
Bush lane ....18, A; 22, B
Butcher row, Ratcliffe ....25, D
    //   //   Camberwell ....33, C
Bute street ....3, C
Butler street ....20, D; 24, A
Buttesland street..18, C
Buxton street ....23, A
Byng street ....26, D
Bywater street ....5, D

Cable street ....25, A
Cadogan place ....3, A; 5, B
    //   street..5, D
    //   terrace...5, D
Caledonia street, Pimlico ....4, D
Caledonian road.................10, C; 13, B; 14, A B D
    //   street..............................13, B; 14, A
Calthorpe place ....5, C
    //   street ....10, C
Calverts street ....25, B
Camera street...5, C
Camberwell road ....33, C; 34 B
    //   New road ....33, C D; 35, C
Cambridge crescent ....13, B
    //   circus.......................................20, C
    //   heath ....20, C; 21, A
    //   place, Edgeware road ....8, A; 9, B
    //   //   Kensington...............................3, D
    //   //   Regent's park ....11, C
    //   road ....20, C D; 23, A
    //   square ....8, A; 9, B
    //   street, Agar-town ....13, B
    //   //   Edgeware road ....8, A; 9, B
    //   //   Golden square ....7, A
    //   //   New North road......................17, C
    //   //   Pimlico ....4, D
    //   //   Great, Hackney road, 19, B; 20, A
    //   //   Little,   do.   19, B; 20, A
    //   terrace, Edgeware road ....8, A; 9, B
    //   //   Liverpool road ....14, D; 16, C
    //   //   Regent's park ....11, C
Camden gardens ....20, D
    //   place, Kensington gardens ....9, C
    //   road ....13, D; 14, C
    //   square ....14, C
    //   street, Bethnal-green ....20, D
    //   //   Camden-town ....13, B
    //   //   Little, do.   ....13, D
    //   //   North, do.   ....13, D
    //   //   Islington ....16, B; 17, A
    //   //   Walworth ....31, B; 33, A; 34, A

Camden terrace, Camden-town ....Plate 13, D
Camomile street ....18, B
Canal bank, Camberwell ....33, C; 34, B
    //   road, Kingsland road ....17, D; 19, A
    //   //   Mile-end road ....23, C; 24, A
    //   //   York road, King's cross.......13, B; 14, A
    //   street, Camberwell................................34, B
    //   terrace, King s road, Camden-town ....13, D
    //   //   York road, King's cross ....13, B
Cancel street..34, B
Canning place, Kensington ....3, D
Cannon place, Whitechapel road ....23, A
    //   row, Westminster ....1, C; 2, A; 4, A
    //   street, City ....18, A; 22, B
    //   //   West, City............1, A; 15, A; 18, A
    //   //   New North road ....17, A
    //   //   St. George's, East.......................25, A
    //   //   road ....23, B; 25, A
Canonbury grove ....16, B; 17, C
    //   lane ....16, C
    //   park, North................................16, D
    //   //   South.......................16, D; 17, C
    //   square ....16, D
    //   street ....16, B; 17, C
    //   terrace ....16, D; 17, C
    //   villas ....16, B; 17, C
Cantelowes road ....14, C
Canterbury place, Walworth ....33, C; 34, A
    //   //   Lambeth road ....35, A
    //   row, Old Kent road ....32, B
    //   terrace, George st., New Kent road, 31, A
    //   //   Lorimore road....................33, C
    //   //   Royal road....................33, C
Canton street ....26, A
Capland street..8, B
Carburton street..7, B
Cardigan street..35, C
Cardington street...11, B
Carey street, Lincoln's Inn Fields............1, B; 6, A
    //   Vincent square ....5, B
Carlisle street, Lambeth ....27, C; 35, B
    //   Portman market ....8, A
    //   Upper, do. ....8, A
    //   Soho square ....6, C; 7, A
    //   Victoria st., Westminster...4, B; 5, B
    //   Winchester st., Bethnal-gn, 20, B; 23, A
Carlton gardens...2, A
    //   hill ....8, D; 12, C
    //   //   East..12, D
    //   place, Carlton hill ....8, D; 12, C
    //   road, Asylum road ....32, B
    //   //   Edgeware road ....8, D; 12, C
    //   square ....32, B
    //   street ....32, B; 34, D
    //   terrace, Battersea road....................36, C
    //   house terrace ....1, D; 2, A
Carnaby street ....7, A
Caroline place, Evelyn street, Deptford.............30, C
    //   //   Kingsland road ....18, C; 20, A
    //   //   Marlborough road, Chelsea, 3, C; 5, D
    //   //   Mecklenburgh square................10, C
    //   //   Moscow road ....9, D
    //   street, Bedford square ....6, D
    //   //   Camden-town ....13, D
    //   //   Coleshill street........................5, B
    //   //   Commercial road, East...23, D; 25, D
    //   //   Old Kent road.......................32, A
    //   //   Regent street, Lambeth ....35, A
Carpenter street..4, A
Carpenter's buildings, London wall ....18, A
Carr street ....23, D
Carter lane, Great ....1, B; 6, A; 15, A
    //   Little ....1, A; 6, A; 15, A
    //   street, Spitalfields ....18, D
    //   Walworth ....33, C; 34, A
Carthusian street ....15, A
Cartwright street..25, A
Cassland road ....21, B; 24, D
Castle lane ....4, B; 5, B

Castle place, Kingsland road ....Plate 20, A
 "   street, Clerkenwell .... 10, B
 "   "   Falcon square ...... 6, A ; 15, A ; 18, A
 "   "   Finsbury .... 15, B ; 18, C
 "   "   Holborn .... 6, A ; 10, A
 "   "   Houndsditch .... 18, B ; 22, A
 "   "   Kent street................ 28, B ; 31, A
 "   "   Leicester square .... 1, D ; 2, B
 "   "   Long Acre .... 2, B ; 6, C
 "   "   Shoreditch.................. 18, D ; 20, B
 "   "   Southwark................................. 27. B
 "   "   East, Oxford street .... 7, A
 "   "   Great,   do.   .... 7, A
 "   "   New, Whitechapel.................... 22, C
 "   "   Old,   do.   .... 22, C
Castor street... 26, A
Catherine street, City road .... 15, D ; 18, C
 "   "   Commercialrd., east,22,C; 23,B; 25,A
 "   "   Pentonville .... 14, B
 "   "   Stafford place, Pimlico .... 4, B
 "   "   Stepney .... 23, D
 "   "   Strand .... 1, D
 "   "   Vauxhall .... 35, D
Causton street... 4, C
Cavendish road .... 12, A
 "   square .... 7, A
 "   street, New North road .... 15, D ; 17, B
 "   "   New, Cavendish square .... 7, B
 "   "   Old,   do.   .... 7, A
Caversham terrace .... 5, C
Centre street... 20, C
Chadwell street .... 10, D ; 15, C
 "   "   Upper .... 10, D
Chalton street .... 11, B
Chamber street, Leman street............... 22, C ; 25, A
 "   "   Stepney .... 23, C
Change alley .... 18, B
Chapel place, Belgrave square .... 2, C
 "   "   Brompton.............................. 3, A
 "   "   Long lane, Bermondsey,27,A; 28,B; 31,A
 "   street, Belgrave square .... 2, C ; 3, A
 "   "   Curtain road .... 18, D
 "   "   Edgeware road .... 8, A
 "   "   Lambs Conduit street .... 10, C
 "   "   Milton street, Cripplegate ...... 15, B
 "   "   Oxford street .... 6, C ; 7, A
 "   "   Park lane .... 2, D
 "   "   Pentonville .... 14, B ; 16, A ; 17, A
 "   "   St. George's, East............ 22, C ; 25, A
 "   "   Somers-town .... 11, B ; 13, A
 "   "   Tottenham-court road .... 7, B
 "   "   Westminster .... 4, B
Chapman street, Upper...................... 22, C ; 25, A
 "   "   Lower.................. 22, C ; 25, A
Chapter street... 4, C
Chancery lane .... 1, B
Chandos street, Cavendish square...................... 7, B
 "   "   Trafalgar square .... 1, D
Charing cross .... 1, D ; 2, B
Charles' lane... 12, B
 "   place, Charles' square............... 15, D ; 18, C
 "   "   Kensington.............................. 3, D
 "   "   Old Kent road .... 32, B
 "   square .... 18, C
 "   street, Back Church lane......... 22, C ; 23, B
 "   "   Berkeley square .... 2, D
 "   "   Blackfriars road .... 27, B
 "   "   Camberwell New road .... 33, D
 "   "   City road .... 15, C
 "   "   New, do. .... 15, C
 "   "   Clarendon square .... 11, B
 "   "   Commercial road, East... 23, D ; 25, C
 "   "   Devonshire st., Mile-end, 20, D ; 23, A
 "   "   Dockhead................................. 28, D
 "   "   Drury lane .... 6, C
 "   "   Eastbourne terrace .... 9, D
 "   "   Ferry road, West .... 26, D
 "   "   Fulham road............................ 5, D

Charles' street, Greenfield street ....Plate 23, B
 "   "   Grosvenor square............. 2, D ; 7, C
 "   "   Hackney road.......................... 20, A
 "   "   New, do. .... 20, A
 "   "   Hackney fields .... 19, B ; 21, A
 "   "   Hampstead road....................... 11, A
 "   "   Hatton garden .... 10, A
 "   "   Haymarket...................... 1, D ; 2, B
 "   "   Horselydown .... 28, A
 "   "   Islington green............. 16, A ; 17, A
 "   "   Kensington .... 3, D
 "   "   Knightsbridge .... 3, B
 "   "   Liverpool road .... 16, A
 "   "   Long acre .... 6, C
 "   "   Lowndes square .... 3, A
 "   "   Manchester square .... 7, D
 "   "   Middlesex hospital .... 7, B
 "   "   Mile-end, New-town .... 23, A
 "   "   New, do. .... 23, A
 "   "   Northampton square .... 15, C
 "   "   Oakley street, Lambeth .... 27, C
 "   "   Old Bethnal green road .... 20, C
 "   "   Old Kent road........................ 32, B
 "   "   Parliament street, Westmin-
 "   "   ster .... 1, C ; 2, A ; 4, A
 "   "   St. George's, East .... 25, A
 "   "   St. John's Wood terrace .... 12, B
 "   "   Soho square .... 6, C ; 7, A
 "   "   Walworth .... 31, B ; 33, A ; 34, A
 "   "   Westminster road......... 27, C ; 35, A
 "   "   Willow walk, Tabernacle sq., ... 18, C
Charlotte place, Mile-end, New-town .... 23, A
 "   row, Mansion house .... 15, B
 "   "   Rotherhithe .... 29, A
 "   street, Bedford square .... 6, D
 "   "   Blackfriars road .... 27, A
 "   "   Great, do. .... 27, C
 "   "   Caledonian road .... 14, B
 "   "   Fitzroy square .... 7, A
 "   "   Upper, do. .... 7, B
 "   "   Old Kent road .... 31, D
 "   "   Old Street road .... 18, C
 "   "   Portland place.............. 7, B ; 11, C
 "   "   Sloane street .... 3, A
 "   "   Stafford row .... 4, B ; 5, B
 "   "   Whitechapel road.................... 23, B
 "   terrace, Copenhagen street............... 14, B
Charlton crescent, Islington .... 16, B
 "   place,   do. ....16, A ; 17, A
 "   street .... 7, B
Charlwood street .... 4, D
Charrington street .... 13, A
Chart street, great .... 18, C
Charter House lane .... 10, B ; 15, A
 "   "   square .... 15, A
 "   "   street............... 10, B ; 15, A
Chatham place, Blackfriars .... 1, B
 "   "   Hackney .... 21, D
 "   "   Walworth .... 31, B ; 33, A
 "   row,   do. .... 31, B
Cheapside .... 6, A ; 15, A ; 22, B
Chelsea market .... 5, C
Cheltenham terrace, King's road, Chelsea .... 5, C
Chenies mews... 6, D
 "   street.. 6, D
Chepstow place, Westbourne grove.................... 9, D
Cherry Garden street .... 28, D
 "   "   " Little .... 28, D
Chesham place, Belgrave square...... 2, C ; 3, A ; 5, B
 "   street .... 5, B
Cheshire street... 20, B ; 23, A
Chester mews.. 2, C ; 3, A
 "   place, Chester square............................... 5, B
 "   "   Green street, Bethnal-green ... 20, D
 "   "   Hyde Park square................... 9, A
 "   "   Regent's park .... 11, D ; 13, C
 "   square .... 5, B
 "   street, Belgrave square ...... 2, C ; 3, A ; 5, B
 "   "   Little   do. .... 2, C ; 3, A

14

Chester street, Green st., Bethnal-green, Plate 20, D
   "   "   Kennington lane .... 33, D; 35, A
   "   terrace, Chester square .... 5, B
   "   "   Regent's park .... 11, D
Chesterfield street, Curzon street, Piccadilly...... 2, D
   "   "   King's cross, 10, C; 11, B; 13, A
   "   "   Great, Marylebone .... 7, B
   "   "   Little, do. .... 7, B
Cheyne row, Great, Chelsea.................5, C
   "   walk,   do.   .... 5. C
Chicksand street .... 23, B
Chigwell hill........................ 25, A
Chilton street .... 30, A
China walk, Lambeth .... 35, A
Chiswell street .... 15, B
Christian street .... 22, C; 25, A
Christopher street, Finsbury .... 15, B
   "   "   Hatton garden .... 10, A
Chryssell road........................ 33, D
Church lane, St. Giles' .... 6, C
   "   "   Limehouse .... 23, D; 25, D; 26, B
   "   "   Whitechapel .... 22, C; 23, B
   "   place, St. Giles' .... 6, C
   "   "   Old Kent road .... 32, A
   "   road, Battersea .... 36, D
   "   "   De Beauvoir-town .... 17, C D
   "   "   Shadwell .... 25, A
   "   "   Stepney .... 25, C
   "   row. Bethnal-green .... 20, B
   "   "   Kennington........................ 33, D; 35, C
   "   street, Blackfriars road .... 27, B
   "   "   Chelsea .... 5, C
   "   "   Grosvenor row, Pimlico .... 5, A
   "   "   Hackney .... 21, D
   "   "   Horselydown .... 28, B
   "   "   Islington .... 16, B; 17, A
   "   "   Kennington .... 35, C
   "   "   Kensington .... 3, D
   "   "   Lambeth .... 35, B
   "   "   Mile-end, New-town .... 23, A
   "   "   Murray street, New North road, 15, D
   "   "   Old Kent road........................ 32, A
   "   "   Paddington .... 8, A; 9, B
   "   "   New, do. .... 8, B
   "   "   Rotherhithe .... 28, C D; 30, A
   "   "   Shoreditch .... 18, D; 20, B
   "   "   Soho .... 6, C; 7, A
   "   "   St. Saviour's, Southwark .... 27, B
   "   "   Spitalfields .... 18, D
   "   "   Trinity square, Southwark ...... 31, A
   "   "   Walworth .... 33, C; 34, A
   "   "   Wapping .... 25, B
   "   "   Waterloo road .... 27, D
   "   "   Westminster .... 4, A
   "   terrace, Walworth road .... 33, C; 34, A
   "   yard row, Newington butts .... 33, B
Churton street .... 4, D
Cinnamon street .... 25, B
Circus, Minories .... 22, D
   "   road........................ 8, D; 12, A C
   "   street .... 8, B
Cirencester place, Fitzroy square .... 7, B
City Garden row, City road .... 15, C
   "   road .... 15, C D; 17, A; 18, C
   "   "   basin, Regent's canal .... 17, A
Clandon street .... 34, A
Clapham road .... 33, D; 35, C
Clapton, Lower........................ 21, D
   "   square .... 21, D
Clara street .... 20, C
Clare market .... 1, B; 6, C
   "   street ....6, C
   "   Hall place........................ 28, D; 30, B
Claremont place, Deptford Lower road...28, D; 30, A
   "   "   Judd street, New road .... 11, B
   "   "   square .... 10, D; 14, B; 16, A
Clarence gardens, Munster street........................ 11, D
   "   place, Clapton square .... 21, D
   "   road, Clapton .... 21, D

Clarence road, Kentish-town road .... Plate 13, D
   "   street, John's row .... 15, C
   "   "   Old Kent road .... 31, D; 34, C
   " . "   Rotherhithe .... 29, B
   "   "   St. Peter's st., Islington, 15, C; 17, A
   "   terrace, Haggerstone........................ 19, B
   "   "   Regent's park .... 11, C; 12, A
Clarendon place, Hyde Park square........................ 9, A
   "   "   Camberwell New road............ 33, C
   "   road .... 3, D
   "   square .... 11, B; 13, A
   "   street, Camberwell New road .... 33, C
   "   "   Clarendon square .... 13, A
   "   "   Little, do. .... 13, A
   "   "   Kent street .... 28, B; 31, A
   "   "   Pimlico .... 4, D
Clarges street........................ 2, D
Clark street .... 23, D
Clark's orchard .... 28, D; 30, A
Clay street .... 7, D
Clayland's road........................ 35, C
Clayton street, Caledonian road .... 14, B
   "   "   Kennington .... 35, C
Cleaver street .... 35, C
Clement's inn .... 1, B; 6, C
   "   lane, Lombard street .... 22, B
   "   "   Strand .... 1, B; 6, A
Clerkenwell close........................ 10, B
   "   green .... 10, B
Cleveland row, Pall Mall........................ 2, A
   "   square .... 9, D
   "   street, Fitzroy square .... 7, B
   "   "   Upper, do. .... 7, B; 11, C
   "   "   Mile-end road .... 23, A
   "   "   Wyndham road .... 33, C
   "   terrace, Cleveland square .... 9, D
Cliff street .... 34, A
Clifford street .... 2, B; 7, A
Clifford's inn .... 1, B; 6, A
Clift street .... 15, D; 17, B
Clifton grove........................ 32, B
   "   road, Abbey road, St. John's wood .... 12, D
   "   "   East,   do. .... 12, D
   "   "   New cross .... 30, D; 32, C
   "   "   Old Kent road .... 32, B
   "   street .... 18, A
   "   "   Upper .... 18, C
   "   villas, Camden New town .... 14, C
Clinger street .... 19, A
Clink street .... 27, B
Clipstone street .... 7, B
Cloak lane .... 18, A; 22, B
Cloth fair .... 10, B; 15, A
Cloudesley square .... 16, A
   "   street........................ 16, A
Club row .... 18, D; 20, B
Coborn road .... 24, B
   "   New road .... 24, B
   "   street .... 24, B
Coburg road .... 31, D; 34, D
   "   row, Westminster .... 4, B
   "   street, Clerkenwell .... 10, D
   "   "   Euston square .... 11, B
   "   "   Rotherhithe .... 30, A
Cochrane terrace, St. John's wood .... 12, A
Cock hill .... 25, D
   "   lane .... 6, A; 10, B; 15, A
Cock and Castle lane .... 19, C
Cockspur street .... 1, D; 2, B
Colchester street........................ 22, C; 23, B
Cold Bath lane .... 21, C
   "   "   square .... 10, C
   "   Blow lane........................ 32, C
Cole street .... 27, A; 31, A
   "   North .... 27, A; 31, A
Coles place .... 27, A; 31, A
Colebrook row, Islington .... 17, A
Coleharbour street .... 20, A
Coleman street, Bank .... 15, B; 18, A

Coleman street, Bunhill row................. Plate 15, D
  "   "   Camberwell ....34, D
  "   "   New North road ....17, A
  "   "   Wapping...............................25, B
Coleshill street .... 5, B
College avenue, Homerton ....21, D
  " grove, Camden-town ....13, B
  " hill, Thames street ....22, B
  " place, Camden-town ....13, B
  " " Chelsea ....5, D
  " " Islington..................................16, A
  " street, Belvedere road ....1, C; 27, C
  " " Chelsea ....5, D
  " " Homerton ....21, D
  " " Islington ....16, C
  " " Thames street ....22, B
  " " Tooley street ....28, A
  " " Great, Camden-town ....13, B D
  " " North,   do.   ....13, D
  " " West,   do.   ....13, B
  " " Great, Westminster..................4, A
  " " Little,   do.   ....4, A
  " terrace, Islington ....16, A
Collier street.......................................14, B
Collier's rents, White street, Borough ....31, A
Collingwood street, Blackfriars road..............27, B
  " " Chelsea ....5. C
  " " Ratcliffe ....25, D
  " " Shoreditch ....18, D; 20, B
  " " Whitechapel road ....23, A
Colonnade ....11, A
Commercial road, East ... 22, C; 23, B D; 25, A C D
  " " Lambeth ....27, D
  " " Limehouse ....26, B
  " " Old Kent road ....32, B
  " " Pimlico .... 5, A
  " street.....................18, B D; 22, C
Compton road ....16, D
  " street, Ball's pond ....17, C
  " " Brunswick square...............11, B
  " " Clerkenwell...........................15, C
  " " Soho...........................6, C; 7, A
  " " New, do.....................6, C; 7, A
Conduit street, New Bond street ....2, B; 7, A
  " " Westbourne terrace..............9, A
Connaught square...................7, D; 8, A; 9, A
  " place, Hyde park ....7, C; 9, A
Constitution hill.......................2, C; 3, A
Coopers road ....31, D; 34, C
  " row, Tower hill ....22, D
Copenhagen place, Limehouse ....23, D; 25, D
  " street......................14, B; 16, A
Coppice row, Clerkenwell ....10, C D
Coram street, Great ....11, A
  " " Little ....11, A
Corbett's court, Spitalfields ....18, D
  " lane..30, B
Cork street ....2, B
Cornbury street ....31, B; 34, C
Cornhill.......................18, B; 22, B
Cornwall place, Holloway road ....14, D
  " road ....27, C D
  " street, Upper...............................25, A
  " " Lower................................25, A
  " terrace, Regent's park ....11, C; 12, A
Corporation row, Clerkenwell ....10, D
Cottage grove, Mile-end road ....24, A
  " lane, City road ....15, C; 17, A
  " " Commercial road, East ... 23, B; 25, C
  " place, Grove street, Deptford ... 29, D; 30, C
  " road ....5, B
  " row, Bermondsey........................28, D
Coulson street ....5, D
Counter street, Borough market......................27, B
  " " Tooley street ....28, A
County terrace, South, New Kent road ....31, B
Court street...23, A
Cousin lane ....22, B
Covent Garden market.........................1, D; 6, C

Coventry street, Bethnal-green .... Plate 20, D
  " " Piccadilly ....1, D; 2, B
Cow lane ....29, A
Cow Cross street ....10, B; 15, A
Cowley street......................................4, A
Cowper street ....15, D; 18, C
Crabtree row, Hackney road ....18, D; 20, A
Craig's court, Charing cross ....1, D
Cranbourne street ....1, D; 2. B; 6, C
Cranbrook street ....20, C; 24, A
Cranmer road ....33, D
Craven hill, Bayswater ....9, D
  " place, do.   ....9, D
  " street, City road ....15, D; 18, C
  " " Strand ....1, D
Crawford street ....7, D; 8, B
Crawley street....................................11, B; 13, A
Cree Church lane ....22, A
Creed lane ....1, B; 6, A; 10, B
Crescent, Belvedere road ....1, C; 27, C
  " Camden road ....14, C
  " Minories ....22, D
  " cottages, Cambridge heath......20, C; 21, A
  " place, Blackfriars..........................10, A
  " " Mornington crescent ....11, D; 13, A
  " road...4, C
  " street ....11, B
Crimscot street......................................31, C
Cripplegate buildings..............................15, B
Crispin street ....18, B
Critchill place, Hoxton ....18, C
Cromer street ....10, C; 11, B
Crompton place, Paddington ....8, A
Cromwell lane.......................................3, C
Cropley street ....15, D
Crosby row, King street, Borough.........27, A; 28, A
  " square..........................18, B; 22, A
Crosier street ....27, C; 35, B
Cross row, Stepney-green ....23, C
  " street, Addington square ....34, B
  " " Ashley crescent ....15, D
  " " Ball's pond road ....17, C
  " " Blackfriars road ....27, B
  " " Carnaby street ....7, A
  " " Church street, Shoreditch............20, B
  " " Commercial road, East ....25, A
  " " Finsbury place ....15, B; 18, A
  " " Green st., Bethnal-green... 20, D; 24, A
  " " Hatcham New town ....32, A
  " " Hatton garden...........................10, A
  " " Islington ....16, B; 17, A
  " " Little, do......................16, B; 17, A
  " " Leonard street, Finsbury ....18, C
  " " Newington butts........................33, B
  " " Poplar ....26, A
  " " Townsend st., Old Kent road,31,B; 34,A
  " " West Ferry road.........................26, D
  " " Westmoreland place, City road ...15, D
  " " Wilderness row, Clerkenwell ......15, C
  " " York road, Lambeth ....27, D
Crown street, Camberwell road ....33, C
  " " Finsbury ....18, A
  " " Old Street road ....18, C
  " " Soho...........................6, C; 7, A
  " " Westminster............ 1, C; 2, A; 4, A
Crucifix lane.......................................28, A
Crutched Friars ....22, D
Cudworth street ....23, A
Culford road.......................................17, D
  " " North ....17, D
Cullum street ....22, B
Cumberland market ....11, D; 13, A
  " place, Addington square...............34, B
  " " Chelsea ....5, D
  " " Hyde park ....7, D
  " street, Brompton..................3, C; 5, D
  " " Goodge street.....................7, B
  " " Hackney road .... 19, B; 20, A
  " " Regent's park ....11, D

Cumberland street, Shoreditch............... Plate 18, D
    ″   ″   Great, Hyde park ...... 7, D; 9, A
    ″   terrace, Lloyd square .... 10, C
    ″   ″   Regent's park ...... 11, D; 13, C
Cumming street .... 14, B
Cunningham place, St. John's Wood road .... 8, B
Cursitor street... 6, A
Curtain road........................ .... 18, C D
Curzon street, New North road .... 15, D
   ″   ″   Piccadilly.................................. 2, D
Cuthbert street .... 8, A
Cutler street .... 18, B; 22, A
Czar street .... 29, D; 30, C

Dacre street .... 4, A
Dalgleish street.................. 23, D; 25, D; 26, B
Dalston green .... 19, C
   ″   lane.......................... 17, D; 19, C D; 21, C
Dame street .... 17, A
Daniel street.. 20, B
Danvers street .... 5, C
Darby street .... 22, D; 25, A
Darling place, Cambridge road .... 23, A
Dartmouth street .... 2, A; 4, A
Davies street .... 2, D; 7, C
Dawson street .... 30, C
Deal street... 23, A
Dean street, Commercial road, East...... 23, B; 25, A
  ″   ″   Fetter lane .... 6, A
  ″   ″   Finsbury .... 15, B
  ″   ″   Holborn .... 6, D
  ″   ″   New North road .... 17, B
  ″   ″   Park lane.................................... 2, D
  ″   ″   Shadwell .... 25, D
  ″   ″   Soho .... 6, C; 7, A
  ″   ″   Little, do.................................. 7, A
  ″   ″   South street, Islington .... 17, A
  ″   ″   Westminster .... 4, A
Dean's buildings, North street, Walworth ...... 31, B
  ″ place,   do.   do. ...... 34, A
  ″ yard, Westminster .... 4, A
De Beauvoir road .... 17, D; 19, A
  ″ square .... 17, D; 19, A
Delamere street... 8, C
Dempsey street .... 23, D
Denbigh place, Pimlico .... 4, D
  ″ street, do. .... 4, D
  ″ terrace, Battersea .... 36, D
Denmark street, Pentonville .... 14, B
  ″   ″ St. George's, East ...... 22, C; 25, A
  ″   ″ Soho .... 6, C; 7, A
Dennett road.. 32, D
Denton street .... 11, B; 13, A
Deptford dockyard.......................... 29, D; 30, C
  ″ lower road .... 28, D; 30. A C
Derby road .... 17, D; 19, A
  ″ street .... 11, B
Derbyshire street .... 20, B
Deverell street... 31, A
Devonport street .... 23, D; 25. C D
Devonshire grove, Old Kent road .... 32, B
  ″ place, Kennington oval .... 35, C
  ″   ″   road .... 35, A
  ″   ″   New road...................... 11, C
  ″ square....................... 18, B; 22, A
  ″ street, Commercial road, East, 23, B; 25, A
  ″   ″ Gloucester square .... 9, B
  ″   ″ Kennington lane .... 35, C
  ″   ″ Lisson grove .... 8, B
  ″   ″ Mile-end ...... 20, D; 23, A; 24, A
  ″   ″ Newington causeway .... 31, A
  ″   ″ New North road ...... 15, D; 17, B
  ″   ″ Portland place .... 7, B; 11, C
  ″   ″ Queen square .... 6, D
  ″ terrace, Cleveland square................ 9, D
Diamond row, Stepney-green .... 23, C
Digby street.. 20, D
Dingle lane .... 26, A
Dock street, Deptford .... 29, D; 30, C

Dock street, London docks .... Plate 22, D; 25, A
Dockhead .... 28, B
Doctors' Commons .... 1, A; 6, A; 10, B
Doctor street, Lower .... 34, B
  ″   ″ Upper .... 34, B
Doddington grove, Surrey gardens ...... 33, D; 34, A
Dorchester place, Blandford square .... 8, B
  ″   street .... 17, B
Doris street .... 35, A
Dorrington street, Clerkenwell .... 10, C
  ″   ″ Leather lane .... 10, A
Dorset place, Dorset square .... 8, B; 11, C
  ″   ″ Liverpool road .... 14, D
  ″   ″ Pall mall .... 1, D
  ″   ″ Pimlico .... 4, C
  ″ square .... 8, B; 11, C
  ″ street, Ball's pond .... 17, C
  ″   ″ Clapham road .... 35, C
  ″   ″ Commercial road, East .... 23, D; 25, D
  ″   ″ Pimlico .... 4, C
  ″   ″ Portman square .... 7, D
  ″   ″ Salisbury square .... 1, B
  ″   ″ Spitalfields .... 18, B
  ″   ″ Upper, Bryanston square ... 7, D; 8, A
  ″   ″   ″ Pimlico .... 4, C
Douglas place, Westbourne grove................... 9, D
  ″ road .... 16, D; 17, C
  ″ street, Lambeth .... 35, B
  ″   ″ Vincent square .... 4, C
Doughty street .... 6, D; 10, C
Dove lane .... 3, C
Dove row, Hackney fields .... 19, B; 20, A; 21, A
Dovedale place, Battersea .... 36, C
Dover place, Dover street .... 2, B
Dover street, Piccadilly .... 2, B
  ″   ″ Great, Borough .... 27, A; 31, A
Dowgate hill .... 22, B
Down street .... 2, D
Downham road .... 17, D; 19, A
Downing street .... 1, C; 2, A; 4, A
Downs' park road .... 19, D; 21, C
Drapers' place, Burton crescent .... 11, B
Draycott place, Chelsea .... 5, D
  ″ street, do. .... 5, D
  ″ terrace, do. .... 5, D
Drummond street .... 11, B
  ″   ″ Little .... 11, B
Drummond's crescent .... 11, B
  ″ road .... 28, D; 30, B
Drury lane .... 1, D; 6, C
Duchess street .... 7, B
Duckett street .... 23, C
Duckett's canal .... 24, A D
Ducking pond row, Whitechapel road .... 23, A
Dudley street .... 6, C; 7, A
Duff street .... 26, A
Duke street, Adelphi .... 1, D; 27, D
  ″   ″ Aldgate .... 22, C
  ″   ″ Bloomsbury .... 6, C
  ″   ″ Chelsea .... 5, C
  ″   ″ Commercial road, Lambeth .... 27, D
  ″   ″ Foley place .... 7, B
  ″   ″ Grosvenor square .... 7, C
  ″   ″ Houndsditch............................ 22, C
  ″   ″ Lincolns Inn Fields .... 6, C
  ″   ″ Lisson grove .... 8, B
  ″   ″ London bridge .... 27, B; 28, A
  ″   ″ Manchester square .... 7, D
  ″   ″ Piccadilly .... 2, B
  ″   ″ St. George's, East .... 25, A
  ″   ″ Spitalfields .... 18, B
  ″   ″ Tyssen street .... 20, B
  ″   ″ Westminster .... 1, C; 2, A; 4, A
  ″   ″ Westminster road... 27, C; 33, B; 35, A
  ″   ″ West Smithfield ...... 6, A; 10, B; 15, A
Duke's row, Euston square .... 11, B
Duncan place, London field .... 21, A
  ″ street, Islington .... 15, C; 17, A
  ″   ″ Whitechapel .... 22, C

Duncan terrace, Islington... Plate 10, D; 15, C; 17, A
Duncannon street .... 1, D
Dnnk street .... 23, B
Dunning's alley, Bishopgate street.................. 22, A
Dunston road .... 19, A
    "   street .... 19, A
Durham place, Chelsea...................................... 5, C
    "   street, Agar-town .... 13, B
    "   "   Chelsea .... 5, C
    "   "   Hackney road .... 20, A
    "   "   Vauxhall gardens .... 35, C
    "   terrace, York square...................... 23, D

Eagle court, St. John's lane .... 15, A
    "   street .... 6, D
    "   Wharf road .... 15, D; 17, B
Earl road .... 31, D
    "   street, Blackfriars .... 1, B
    "   "   Edgeware road .... 8, B
    "   "   Finsbury .... 18, A
    "   "   London road .... 33, B; 35, A
    "   "   Millbank .... 4, A
    "   "   Seven Dials .... 6, C; 7, A
East lane, Bermondsey .... 28, D
    "   place, Hackney .... 21, D; 24, C
    "   road, Hoxton .... 15, D; 18, C
    "   Smithfield .... 22, D; 25, A
    "   "   Lower .... 22, D
    "   street, Caledonian road .... 14, A
    "   "   Cambridge heath .... 20, C; 21, B
    "   "   Globe fields .... 24, A
    "   "   Goldsmiths' row .... 20, A
    "   "   Green street, Bethnal-green, 20, D; 24, A
    "   "   Hoxton .... 18, C
    "   "   Kennington road .... 35, A
    "   "   Lamb's Conduit street .... 6, D
    "   "   Manchester square.................... 7, D
    "   "   Walworth .... 31, B; 33, A C; 34, A C
    "   Harding street .... 1, B; 6, A
    "   India Dock road .... 26, A
    "   Mount street . ... 23, B
    "   and West India Dock cottages .... 26, A
Eastcheap .... 22, B
Eastbourne terrace .... 8, A; 9, B D
Eastfield street .... 23, D
Easton street.. 10, C
Eaton lane, North .... 5, B
    "   "   South .... 5, B
    "   place, Eaton square.............................. 5, B
    "   "   West, do. .... 5, B
    "   row,   do.   .... 5, B
    "   square .... 5, B
    "   street, Lambeth .... 27, C D
    "   "   Pimlico .... 5, B
Ebenezer row, Kennington lane .... 33, B; 35, A
Ebury square.. 5, A
    "   street .... 5, B
    "   "   Little .... 5, A
    "   "   Upper.................................. 5, A B
Eccleston place, Pimlico .... 5, B
    "   square .... 4, D
    "   street .... 5, B
    "   "   East .... 5, B
    "   "   South .... 5, B
    "   "   Upper .... 2, C; 5, B
Eden grove, Holloway .... 14, D
Edgeware road .... 7, C; 8, A D; 9, A B; 12, C
Edith street .... 19, B; 20, A
Edmund street .... 13, B
Edward street, Albany street .... 11, D; 13, A C
    "   "   Little, do. .... 11, D
    "   "   Barnsbury road .... 14, B
    "   "   Belvedere road, Lambeth .... 27, C
    "   "   Bermondsey .... 28, B; 31, A
    "   "   Bethnal-green .... 20, B
    "   "   Blackfriars road .... 27, B
    "   "   Caledonian road .... 14, D
    "   "   Dockhead .... 28, C
    "   "   Hampstead road .... 11, B; 13, A

Edward street, Hoxton .... Plate 19, A
    "   "   Kingsland road .... 18, C; 20, B
    "   "   Lower Kennington lane .... 35, A
    "   "   Portman square .... 7, D
    "   "   St. John's Wood terrace............ 12, B
    "   "   Salmon's lane .... 23, D; 25, D
    "   "   Soho .... 6, C; 7, A
    "   "   Stepney .... 23, C
    "   "   Surrey gardens .... 33, D; 34, A
    "   "   Vincent square .... 4, C
    "   "   Wharf road, City road .... 15, D
    "   "   York road, Battle bridge, 13, B; 14, A
Edward's place, Maida hill.............................. 8, A
    "   street .... 30, D; 32, C
Elder walk, Islington...................................... 17, A
    "   street .... 18, D
Eldon road .... 3, C
    "   street .... 18, A
Elgin road .... 8, D; 12, C
Eli street .... 19, A
Elim street .... 28, B; 31, A
Eliza place, Sadler's wells.............................. 10, D
Elizabeth street, Hackney road .... 20, A
    "   "   Liverpool road .... 16, A
    "   "   Pimlico .... 5, B
    "   "   South, do. .... 5, A B
    "   "   St. George's, East ...... 22, C; 25, A
    "   "   Walworth .... 33, C; 34, B
Ellen street .... 22, C; 25, A
Elliot's row, St. George's road .... 33, B
Ellis street .... 5, B
Elm street .... 10, C
Elm-tree place, Paddington .... 8, A
    "   "   road .... 8, D; 12, C
Elms lane.. 9, C D
Elstree street .... 13, B
Eltham street .... 31, B; 33, A; 34, A
Ely place, Holborn .... 6, A; 10, A
    "   "   Hoxton .... 19, A
    "   "   St. George's road .... 33, B; 35, A
    "   "   South Lambeth New road .... 35, C
Emerson street .... 1, A; 27, B
Emma street .... 20, C; 21, A
Emmett street .... 26, B
Endell street .... 6, C
Endsleigh street .... 11, A
Enfield road .... 17, D; 19, A
    "   "   North .... 17, D
Englefield road .... 17, D; 19, C
Ennislie place, Hyde park .... 3, D
Epping place, Mile-end.................................. 23, A
Ernest street, Bermondsey .... 28, B; 31, C
    "   "   Mile-end road .... 23, C
    "   "   Regent's park .... 11, D
Esher street, Millbank .... 4, C
    "   "   Upper Kennington lane .... 35, C
Essex street, Bethnal-green road .... 20, B
    "   "   Cambridge road .... 20, D; 23, A
    "   "   Commercial road, East ...... 22, C; 23, B
    "   "   Green street, Bethnal-green ...... 20, D
    "   "   Kingsland road .... 18, C; 19, A
    "   "   Southwark .... 27, B
    "   "   Strand .... 1, B; 6, A
    "   "   Vincent terrace, City road, 15, C; 17, A
Europa place, Battersea.................................. 36, D
Euston square .... 11, A B
Evans street .... 26, A
Evelyn row, Deptford .... 29, D; 30, C
    "   street, do. .... 30, C
    "   "   New North road .... 15, D
Everett street .... 6, D; 11, A
Everilda street .... 14, B
Eversholt street .... 13, A
Ewer street .... 27, A
Ewhurst street .... 34, A
Exeter street, Kentish-town road .... 13, D
    "   "   Lisson grove .... 8, B
    "   "   Sloane street.......................... 3, A
    "   "   Strand .... 1, D

Exmouth street, Clerkenwell .... Plate 10, C D
　　〃　　　〃　Commercial road, East, 23, D; 25, C
　　〃　　　〃　Hampstead road .... 11, B
Eyre street .... 10, A

Fair place, Stepney .... 23, D
　〃　street, Horselydown .... 28, A
　〃　〃　Stepney .... 23, D
Falcon square .... 6, A; 15, A; 18, A
　〃　street .... 6, A; 10, B; 15, A
Fann street .... 15, A
Farm street .... 2, D
Farmer street .... 25, B
Farringdon market .... 1, B; 6, A; 10, A
　〃　street .... 1, B; 6, A; 10, A
Farthing street .... 20, B
Fashion street, Dockhead .... 28, B
　〃　〃　Spitalfields .... 18, B
Featherstone buildings, Holborn .... 6, D; 10, A
　〃　〃　Limehouse .... 23, D
　〃　street .... 15, D
Felix street, Hackney road .... 20, C
　〃　〃　Lambeth .... 27, C; 35, B
Fell street .... 15, B
Fellows street .... 19, B
Felton street .... 17, B
Fenchurch street .... 22, B D
Fendall street .... 31, C
Fentiman road .... 35, C
Fenton street, Upper .... 22, C; 23, B; 25, A
　〃　〃　Lower .... 22, C
Ferdinand place, Hampstead road .... 13, D
　〃　street,　do.　.................... 13, D
Ferry road, West, Isle of Dogs .... 26, D
　〃　street .... 35, B
Fetter lane .... 1, B; 6, A; 10. A
Field lane .... 6, A; 10, B
Fieldgate street .... 23, B
Finch lane .... 18, B; 22, B
　〃　street .... 23, B
Finchley place, Finchley road........................ 12, D
　〃　road .... 12, D
Finsbury circus .... 15, B; 18, A
　〃　place .... 15, B; 18, A
　〃　market .... 18, D
　〃　square .... 15, B; 18, A
　〃　street .... 15, B
First street .... 3, C; 5, D
Fish street hill .... 22, B
Fitzroy road .... 13, C
　〃　square .... 7, B; 11, A
　〃　street .... 7, B
　〃　〃　Upper .,...................................... 11, A
Flask lane, Ebury square .... 5, A
　〃　row,　do.　.. 5, A
Fleet lane .... 1, B; 6, A; 10, B; 15, A
　〃　street, Bethnal-green .... 20, B; 23, A
　〃　〃　City .... 1, B; 6, A; 10, A
Fleming road .... 33, C D
　〃　street .... 19, A
Flint street .... 31, B; 34, A
Flower and Dean street .... 18, B
Fludyer street .... 1, C; 2, A; 4 A
Foley place, Great Portland street .... 7, B
　〃　street .... 7, B
Ford road .... 24, B
　〃　street .... 24, B
Fore street, Cripplegate .... 15, B; 18, A
　〃　〃　Limehouse .... 26, B
　〃　〃　Lower, Lambeth .... 35, B
　〃　〃　Upper,　do.　...................... 35, B D
Forest row, Dalston .... 17, D; 19, C; 21, C
Forston street .... 15, D; 17, B
Fort street, Bermondsey .... 31, C
　〃　〃　Spitalfields .... 18, D
Foster lane .... 6, A; 15, A; 18, A; 22, B
　〃　street, Bishopsgate .... 18, B
　〃　〃　Whitechapel .... 23, A
Fox's buildings, Kent street, Borough .... 31, A

Fox's lane .... Plate 25, B
Foxley road .... 33, D
Francis street, Chelsea .... 5, D
　〃　〃　Hoxton .... 17, B
　〃　〃　Newington butts .... 33, B; 34, A
　〃　〃　Tottenham-court road ...... 6, D; 7, B
　〃　〃　Westminster .... 4, B
　〃　〃　Westminster road .... 27, C; 35, A
Frances street, Vauxhall .... 35, C
Frazier street .... 27, C
Frederick place, Mile-end road .... 24, A
　〃　〃　Newington butts .... 33, B; 34, A
　〃　street, Albany street, Regent's park, 11, C
　〃　〃　Bermondsey .... 28, D
　〃　〃　Gray's Inn road .... 10, C
　〃　〃　Hampstead road .... 11, B
　〃　〃　Limehouse .... 23, D; 25, D
　〃　〃　Townshend rd., Regent's pk., 12, B
　〃　〃　Vincent square .... 4, C
Freeling street .... 14, B
Friar street .... 27, A
Friday street .... 1, A; 15, A; 22, B
Friendly place, White Horse lane .... 23, C
Frith street .... 6, C; 7, A
Frog lane .... 17, A
Fulham place, Harrow road .... 8, A
　〃　road .... 3, C; 5, D
Fuller street .... 20, B
Fulwood's rents, Holborn .... 6, B
Furnival's Inn .... 6, B; 10, A

Gainsford street, Horselydown .... 28, A
　〃　〃　Islington .... 14, B
Galway street .... 15, D
Garden road .... 8, D
　〃　row, London road........................ 33, B; 35, A
　〃　street, Stepney .... 23, D
　〃　〃　Vauxhall bridge road .... 4, C
　〃　〃　Upper, do. .... 4, C
　〃　〃　Great, Whitechapel .... 23, B
Gardeners lane .... 1, C; 2, A; 4, A
Garford street .... 26, B
Garlick hill .... 1, A; 22, B
Garnault place, New River head .... 10, D
Garway road .... 9, D
Gascoigne place, Virginia row........................ 20, B
Gascoyne road .... 24, D
Gate street .... 6, C
Gates street .... 26, A
Gaywood street .... 33, B
Gedling street .... 28, B
Gee street, Clarendon square .... 11, B
　〃　〃　Goswell street .... 15, C
George gardens, Bethnal-green road .... 20, B
　〃　place, Battersea .... 36, D
　〃　〃　Globe fields.......................... 20, D
　〃　〃　Russell street, Bermondsey ...... 28, B
　〃　row, Bermondsey .... 28, D
　〃　square, Hoxton .... 18, C
　〃　street, Andrew's road .... 21, A
　〃　〃　Battle bridge.......................... 10, C
　〃　〃　Blackfriars road .... 27, B
　〃　〃　Bloomsbury .... 6, C
　〃　〃　Brandon st., Walworth,31,B;33,A;34,A
　〃　〃　Chelsea............................ 5, A
　〃　〃　Commercial road, East .... 25, D
　〃　〃　Foley place .... 7, B
　〃　〃　Great Suffolk street.................. 27, A
　〃　〃　Great Union street .... 33, B
　〃　〃　Hampstead road .... 11, A B
　〃　〃　Hanover square .... 7, A
　〃　〃　Harmood street, Hampstead road, 13, D
　〃　〃　Holloway .... 14, D
　〃　〃　Horsemonger lane .... 31, A
　〃　〃　Kent st., Borough, 27, A; 28, B; 31, A
　〃　〃　London field .... 21, A
　〃　〃　Minories .... 22, C
　〃　〃　New North road .... 17, C
　〃　〃　Old Bethnal-green road .... 20, D

George street, Old Kent road .... Plate 32, B
    "   " Old Montague street .... 23, B
    "   " Oxford street .... 7, C
    "   " Portman square .... 7, D
    "   " Upper, do. .... 7, D; 8, A; 9, B
    "   " Pentonville............................. 14, B
    "   " Princes road, Kennington .... 35, A
    "   " Richmond street, Walworth ..... 34, A
    "   " Rotherhithe .... 29, B; 30, A
    "   " Salmon's lane .... 23, D; 25, D
    "   " Spitalfields .... 20, B; 23, A
    "   " Stepney .... 23, D
    "   " Vauxhall walk .... 35, B
    "   " Whitechapel .... 22, C
    "   " Wyndham road...................... 33, C
    "   " Great, Bermondsey......... 28, B; 31, C
    "   "   " Westminster, 1, C; 2, A; 4, A
    "   " Little, Buckingham row, do. .... 4, B
    "   "   " Bermondsey.... 28, B; 31, C
    "   "   " Hampstead road .... 11, B
    " yard, Lombard street .... 22, B
    "   " Oxford street............................. 7, C
    "   " Whitechapel .... 22, C
George's place, Holloway .... 14, D
    " row, St. Luke's .... 15, D
Georgiana street .... 13, D
Gerrard street, Islington .... 15, C; 17, A
    "   " Soho .... 2, B; 6, C
Gibraltar row, St. George's road .... 33, B; 35, A
    " walk, Bethnal-green...................... 20, B
Gibson square .... 16, A
    " street................................... 27, C
Gifford street .... 19, A
Gilbert street, Clare market .... 6, C
    "   " Oxford street .... 7, C
Gill street .... 26, B
Gillingham street .... 4, D; 5, A
Giltspur street .... 6, A; 10, B; 15, A
Gladstone street.............................. 33, B; 35, A
Glasshouse street, London dock............ 22, D; 25, A
    "   " Ratcliffe .... 25, D
    "   " Vauxhall........................ 35, D
    " yard, Goswell street.................... 15, A
Glebe place, King's road, Chelsea...................... 5, C
Glengall grove, Old Kent road .... 31, D; 34, D
    " street................................ 26, D
    " terrace, Glengall grove .... 34, D
Globe fields .... 23, C; 24, A
    " road .... 20, D; 23, C
    " street, Bethnal-green...................... 20, D
    "   " Rotherhithe...................... 29, A
    "   " Wapping .... 25, B
Gloucester crescent, Bayswater...................... 9, D
    "   " Regent's park .... 13, D
    " gardens, Bishops' road .... 9, D
    " grove, Brompton .... 3, C
    "   " West, do............................. 3, C
    " place, Albany road, Camberwell ..... 34, D
    "   " Camden-town .... 13, A B
    "   " Gloucester crescent, do........ 13, D
    "   " Hackney road .... 20, A; 21, A
    "   " Hyde park .... 9, D
    "   " Portman square .... 7, D; 8, B
    "   " Upper .... 8, B; 11, C; 12, A
    " road, Bermondsey .... 31, D; 32, A
    "   " Kensington........................ 3, C D
    "   " Regent's park .... 13, C
    " row, Camberwell.......................... 34, D
    "   " Walworth .... 31, B: 33, A
    " square .... 8, A; 9, B
    " street, Bayham street .... 13, A
    "   " Cambridge heath ...... 20, C; 21, A
    "   " Commercial road, East, 22, C; 23, B
    "   " Curtain road .... 18, D
    "   " Hackney road .... 20, A; 21, A
    "   " Haggerstone .... 19, B
    "   " North, do............................ 19, B
    "   " West, do............................. 19, B
    "   " Hoxton .... 18, C; 19, A

Gloucester street, New, Hoxton ... Plate 18, C; 19, A
    "   " Oakley st., Lambeth, 27, C; 35. A
    "   " Pimlico .... 4, D
    "   " West, do............................. 4, D
    "   " Portman square .... 7, D
    "   " Upper, do............................. 8, B
    "   " Queen square .... 6, D
    "   " Regent's park..................... 13, C D
    "   " St. John street road............. 10, D
    "   " Vauxhall walk .... 35, D
    " terrace, Bayswater .... 9, D
    "   " Hoxton .... 19, A
    "   " Regent's park .... 13, C
    "   " Walworth .... 33, C
Godfrey street.. 5, D
Golden lane .... 15, A
    " square .... 2, B; 7, A
Golden's place, Kennington lane............... 35, A
Goldington crescent .... 13, B
    " street........................... 13, B
Goldsmiths' row, Hackney road, 19, B; 20, A; 21, A
Gomm road .... 30, A
Goodge street .... 6, D; 7, B
Goodman's stile .... 23, B
    " yard .... 22, D
Goodwin street.. 14, D
Gordon place, Gordon square .... 11, A
    " square .... 6, D; 11, A
    " street, Gordon square .... 11, A
    "   " City road .... 15, C; 17, A
Goring street .... 21, A
Gossett street .... 20, B
Goswell road .... 15, C; 16, A; 17, A
    " street .... 15, A C
    " terrace, Goswell road .... 15, C
Gough square .... 1, B; 6, A
    " street................................. 10, C
Gould's hill, Shadwell .... 25, D
Goulston street.. 22, C
Gower place, Euston square...................... 11, A
    " street .... 6, D
    "   " North....................... 11, A
    "   " Upper .... 6, D; 11, A
Gower's walk .... 22, C; 23, B; 25, A
Grace street .... 14, B
Gracechurch street .... 22, B
Grafton crescent .... 13, D
    " place, Euston square .... 11, B
    " street, Bond street .... 2, B
    "   " Fitzroy square .... 7, B; 11, A
    "   " East, do.................... 7, B; 11, A
    "   " Soho .... 2, B; 6, C; 7, A
Graham street, City road.................. 15, C; 17, A
    "   " Pimlico .... 5, A
Granby street, Bethnal-green .... 20, B
    "   " Hampstead road .... 11, D; 13, A
    "   " Waterloo road .... 27, C
Grand Junction road .... 8, A; 9, B
Grange, The, Bermondsey .... 28, B; 31, C
    " place, Deptford Lower road............ 30, A
    " road, Bermondsey .... 28, B; 31, C
    "   " Upper, do. .... 31, C D; 34, C
    "   " Canonbury...................... 16, D
    "   " Dalston .... 19, C
    "   " Hampstead road .... 13, D
    " street .... 31, D
    " walk, Bermondsey .... 28, B; 31, C
    "   " Hoxton .... 17, B
Granville square .... 10, C
Gravel lane, Houndsditch .... 18, B; 22, C
    "   " Southwark...................... 27, A B
    "   " New, Wapping................... 25, B
    "   " Old,   do. .... 25, B
Gray street, Blackfriars road .... 27, A C
    " Duke street, Manchester square..... 7, C
Gray's Inn .... 6, B; 10, A
    " lane.............................. 6, B; 10, A
    " road .... 6, B; 10, C; 11, B
Great Dover street .... 27, A; 28, B; 31, A

Great Hermitage street .... Plate 22, D; 25, B
" St. Helen's .... 18, B; 22, A
" turnstile .... 6, C
Greek street, Soho.......................... 6, C; 7, A
Green Arbour court, Old Bailey .... 1, B; 15, A
" Bank, Tooley street .... 28, A
" " Wapping .... 25, B
Green park.. 2, C
" street, Bethnal-green .... 20, D; 24, A
" " Blackfriars road .... 27, A; 33, B
" " Church street, do. .... 27, B
" " Globe road .... 23, C
" " Grosvenor square .... 7, C; 9, A
" " Kennington .... 33, D; 34, A
" " Leicester square .... 2, B
" " London hospital...................... 23, B
" " Marlborough road, Chelsea, 3, C; 5, D
" " Stepney .... 23, D
" " Theobald's road .... 6, D
" terrace, New River head.................. 10, D
Green walk, Holland street, Blackfriars ...1, A; 27, B
Green's row, Chelsea....................................5 C
Greenfield street.............................. 22, C; 23, B
Greenhill's rents, Smithfield bars .... 10, B
Greenland place, Judd street .... 11, B
Green-man's lane................................... 16, B
Greenwood's rents, Well street, Hackney ...... 21, B
Grenville street, Brunswick square .... 6, D; 11, A
" " Clarendon square .... 11, B; 13, A
Gresham street...................... 10, B; 15, A B; 18, A
Greville place, Edgeware road .... 8, D; 12, D
" road .... 12, D
" street .... 6, B; 10, A
Grey Coat place, Westminster .... 4, A
" " street, do. .... 4, A
" Eagle street................................... 18, D
Griffin street, Shadwell .... 25, B
" " York road, Lambeth.................. 27, C
Grocers' Hall court, Poultry............... 15, B; 22, B
Grosvenor canal and basin .... 4, D, 5, A
" crescent, Belgrave square .... 2, C; 3, A
" mews .... 2, D; 7, A
" park .... 33, C
" place, Bethnal-green .... 20, D
" " Camberwell .... 33, C
" " Hyde park............. 2, C; 3, A; 5, B
" " St. George's, Camberwell ...... 34, D
" row, Pimlico .... 5, A B
" square .... 7, C
" street, Camberwell road ...... 33, C; 34, B
" " Commercial road, East, 23, D; 25,C
" " Grosvenor square............. 7, A C
" " Upper, do. .... 2, D; 7, C; 9, A
" " Islington .... 15, D; 17, A
" " Millbank .... 4, C
" " West, Eaton square ... 2, C; 5, B
Grove, The, Caledonian road .... 14, D
" " Hackney......................... 21, C
" " South Lambeth .... 35, D
" " Southwark.......................... 27, B
" cottages, Holloway.................. 14, D
" lane, Hackney .... 21, B; 24, D
" " Waterloo road .... 27, C
" place, Brompton road .... 3, A
" " Hackney .... 21, C
" " Mile-end .... 23, A
" road, Mile-end road .... 20, C; 21, B; 24, A
" " St. John's wood......................... 8, B
" street, Bethnal-green...................... 20, D
" " Camden-town .... 13, D
" " Commercial road, East 22,C; 23,B; 25,A
" " Lower, do. .... 22, C
" " Deptford Dockyard .... 29, D
" " Hackney................... 21, B; 24, C
" " Holloway............................ 14, D
" " Islington .... 16, B
" " Mile-end road.................... 24, A
" " Poplar .... 26, A
" " Walworth, ... 34, C

Grove terrace, Regent st., Mile-end road, Plate 23, C
Grove End road .... 8, B D; 12, C
Grundy street .... 26, A
Guildford place, Clerkenwell .... 10, C
" " Foundling hospital .... 6, D; 10, C
" street, Belvedere road .... 27, C
" " Russell square.. 6, D; 10, C; 11, A
" " Little, do. .... 6, D; 11, A
" " Great, Southwark.......... 1, A; 27, B
" " Little, do. .... 27, A
" " Walworth .... 34, A
" " East, Clerkenwell .... 10, C
Gun alley, Bermondsey street...................... 28, B
" " Wapping .... 25, B
" lane .... 26, B
" street .... 18, B D
Gutter lane............................... 10, B; 15, A; 22, B
Guy street.. 28, B

Haberdashers' street .... 18, C
" walk .... 18, C
Hackney common .... 21, B
" downs .... 21, C
" road .... 18, D; 20, A C; 21, A
" road crescent .... 20, A
" terrace, Cassland road............ 21, B; 24, C
Haggerstone lane .... 19, A B
Hague street .... 20, B
Hale street, New North road .... 17, B
" " Poplar .... 26, A
Hale's place, South Lambeth .... 35, D
Halfpenny hatch .... 29, B; 30, A
Halfmoon crescent, Pentonville .... 14, B
" street, Bishopsgate .... 18, B; 22, A
" " Piccadilly .... 2, D
" " Whitechapel .... 22, C
Halifax street .... 23, B
Halkin street .... 2, C; 3, A
" terrace .... 3, A
Hall place, Church street, Paddington .... 8, A
" " St. John's wood .... 8, D; 12, C
" street .... 15, C
Halliford street .... 17, C
Halsey street .... 3, A; 5, D
Halton street .... 16, B; 17, A B
Hamilton mews, North .... 12, C
" place, Piccadilly.................. 2, C D; 3, A
" row, Battle bridge .... 10, C; 14, B
" street, Camden-town .... 13, D
" " Deptford .... 30, D; 32, C
" " Wandsworth road .... 36, A
" terrace, St. John's wood .... 8, D; 12, C
" " Upper, do.................. 8, D; 12, C
Hampden street............................ 11, B; 13, A
Hampstead road .... 11, A B; 13, A D
" " New .... 13, D
Hampton street .... 33, A B; 34, A
Han's place, Chelsea .... 3, A
" street, do.. 3, A
Hanover cottages, Park rd., Regent's park 8, B; 12, A
" gate, Regent's park .... 12, A
" place, Clapham road .... 35, C
" " Regent's park ...... 8, B; 11, C; 12, A
" square .... 7, A
" street, Bermondsey .... 28, B; 31, C
" " Hanover square .... 7, A
" " Islington .... 15, C; 17, A
" " Long acre .... 6, C
" " Pimlico .... 4, D
" " Rotherhithe .... 29, B
" " Walworth road .... 33, A; 34, A
" terrace, Regent's park .... 12, A
Hannibal road................................... 23, C
Hanway street .... 6, C; 7, A
Harcourt street .... 8, B
Hardinge street, Commercial road, East ...... 25, C D
" " Islington .... 16, A
Hardington street................................ 8, A
Hare court, Aldersgate street .... 15, A

Hare street............................... Plate 20, B; 23, **A**
    " walk, Kingsland road .... 19, A
Harewood place, Hanover square .... 7, A
    "   *"* Lisson grove .... 8, B
    " square .... 8, B
Harley street, Battersea .... 36, C
    "   *"* Bow road .... 24, B
    "   *"* Cavendish square .... 7, B
    "   *"* Upper, do. ....7, B; 11, C
Harleyford road..................................... 35, C D
    " street .... 35, C
Harmood street .... 13, D
Harp alley, Farringdon street .... 6, A
    " lane .... 22, D
Harper street .... 31, A B
Harpur street .... 6, D
Harrington square .... 11, B D; 13, A
    " street .... 11, D; 13, A
Harris's court, Brook street, Ratcliff .... 25, D
Harrison street .... 10, C; 11, B
Harrod street .... 20, C; 24, A
Harrow alley, Middlesex street, Whitechapel... 22, A
    " road .... 8, A C; 9, B
    " street .... 8, B
Hart street, Bloomsbury .... 6, D
    "   *"* Covent garden................. 2, B; 6, C
    "   *"* Cripplegate .... 10, B; 15, B
    "   *"* Crutched friars .... 22, D
Hart's lane .... 20, B
Hartland road .... 13, D
Harvey street .... 17, B
Hasker street .... 3, C; 5, D
Hasting's street .... 11, B
Hatcham road .... 32, A
    " street .... 32, A
    " Park road .... 32, D
Hatfield street, Goswell street .... 15, A
    "   *"* Blackfriars .... 27, D
Hatton garden .... 6, A B; 10, A
    " street .... 8, A
    " wall .... 10, A
Havering street .... 23, D; 25, C
Haverstock hill .... 13, D
Haward street .... 36, A
Hawkins street...................................... 23, B
Hawley crescent .... 13, D
    " road .... 13, D
Hay hill .... 2, B D
    " street .... 19, B; 20, A; 21, A
Hay's lane .... 28, A
    " mews, Berkeley square .... 2, D
Haydon square .... 22, C
Hayes place, Islington .... 16, B; 17, A
Hayfield place, Stepney green...................... 23, C
Haymarket ....1, D; 2, B
Heath street............................33, D; 25, C
Heathcote street .... 10, C
Heddon street, ... 2, B
Helen's place, Green street, Bethnal-green...... 20, D
Helmet row, St. Luke's............................. 15, C
Helmsley place, London field .... 21, A
    " street, do. .... 21, A
Hemingford road .... 14, B
Hemming's row ....1, D; 2, B
Hemsworth street .... 19, A
Hen and chicken lane .... 31, B D; 34, C
Hendre road ....31, D; 34, C
Heneage lane .... 22, A
    " street .... 23, B
Henrietta street, Brunswick square .... 11, B
    "   *"* Cavendish square .... 7, A
    "   *"* Covent garden .... 1, D
    "   *"* Hackney road .... 20, A
    "   *"* Manchester square .... 7, C
Henry street, Bedford square, East.................. 23, B
    "   *"* Gray's Inn road .... 6, D
    "   *"* Hampstead road .... 11, A
    "   *"* Kennington lane .... 35, C
    "   *"* Kent street, Borough .... 31, A

Henry street, Limehouse .... Plate 23, D; 25, D
    "   *"* Marlborough road, Chelsea......... 5, D
    "   *"* Old Kent road .... 3z, D
    "   *"* Pentonville .... 10, D; 14, B
    "   *"* Regent's park........................ 12, B
    "   *"* St. Luke's........................... 15, D
    "   *"* Stepney............................ 23, C
Henstridge villas, St. John's wood................. 12, B
Herbert street, Great Cambridge street, 19, B; 20, A
    "   *"* New North road..................... 15, D
Hercules buildings, Lambeth............ 27, C; 35, A B
Hereford road....................................... 9, D
    " square .... 3, C
    " street, Bethnal-green .... 20, B; 23, A
    "   *"* Lisson grove .... 8, B
    "   *"* Park lane .... 7, C; 9, A
Hermes street .... 10, D; 14, B
Hertford place, Haggerstone .... 19, A B
    " road .... 17, D; 19, A C
    " street, Fitzroy square .... 7, B; 11, A
    "   *"* Haggerstone .... 19, A B
    "   *"* Park lane .... 2, D
    "   *"* Somers-town .... 11, B
Hickman's folly, Dockhead .... 28, D
High Holborn .... 6, C; 10, A
High street, Aldgate .... 22, C
    "   *"* Borough .... 27, A B; 28, A
    "   *"* Camden-town .... 13, D
    "   *"* Homerton .... 21, D
    "   *"* Hoxton Old town... 17, B; 18, C; 19, A
    "   *"* Islington.............. 15, C; 16, A; 17, A
    "   *"* Kensington........................ 3, D
    "   *"* Lambeth........................... 35, B
    "   *"* Marylebone .... 7, B D; 11, C
    "   *"* Mile-end New town................ 23, B
    "   *"* Newington—*See Newington butts*... 33, B
    "   *"* Notting hill....................... 9, C
    "   *"* Poplar............................ 26, A
    "   *"* Portland town .... 12, A
    "   *"* St. Giles' .... 6, C; 7, A
    "   *"* Shadwell .... 25, B D
    "   *"* Shoreditch—*See Shoreditch* 18, D; 20, B
    "   *"* Stepney .... 23, D
    "   *"* Vauxhall .... 35, D
    "   *"* Wapping .... 22, D; 25, B; 28, C
    "   *"* Whitechapel .... 22, C; 23, B
Highbury crescent .... 16, C
    " grove .... 16, D
    " place .... 16, C
    " terrace .... 16, C
Hill road .... 12, C
    " street, Berkeley square .... 2, D
    "   *"* Blackfriars road .... 27, A
    "   *"* Finsbury...................... 15, B; 18, C
    "   *"* Knightsbridge.................... 3, A B
    "   *"* Peckham .... 34, D
    "   *"* Walworth road .... 33, C; 34, B
Hinde street .... 7, D
Hindel street .... 19, C
Hindon street .... 4, D
Hinton street .... 20, D
Hodson street .... 33, B; 34, A
Holborn hill .... 6, A; 10, A
Holford square.............................. 10, C; 14, B
Holland grove, Vassal road .... 33, D
    " street, Blackfriars .... 1, A; 27, B
    "   *"* Clapham road .... 35, C
    "   *"* Westminster..................... 4, A
Holles street .... 7, A
Holloway road .... 14, D; 16, C
Holly street, North .... 19, C
    "   *"* South .... 19, A C
Holly-bush gardens .... 20, D
    " place .... 20, D
Holmes street .... 23, D
Holt place, Hoxton.................................. 17, B
Holywell lane .... 18, D; 20, B
    " row .... 18, C
    " street, Millbank .... 4, A

Holywell street, Strand............... Plate 1, B; 6, C
Homer row, New road,............................8, A
    " street, Lambeth................................35, B
    " *"* New road ....8, A
Homerton, Upper ....21, D
    " row...21, D
    " terrace, Morning lane....................21, D
Hooper square...22, C
Hooper's street ....27, C; 35, A
Hope street, Hackney road ....20, C
    " *"* Holloway ....14, D
    " *"* Spitalfields ....18, D; 20, B
    " town...................................20, B
Hopkins street ....7, A
Horace street ....35, D
Horny lane..31, C
Horseferry road, Westminster..........................4, A
    " Branch road, Limehouse ......23, D; 25, D
Horselydown lane ....28, A
Horsemonger lane ....27, A; 31, A; 33, A
Hosier lane.............................6, A; 10, B; 15, A
Houghton street ....1, B; 6, C
Houndsditch ....18, B; 22, A C
Howard street ....1, B
Howland street..7, B
Howley place, Maida hill................................8, C
Hoxton square...18, C
Hugh street ....4, D; 5, A
Hull street..15, C
Hungerford bridge ....1, C; 27, D
    " market ....1, D
    " street, Commercial rd. East, 23, B; 25, A
    " *"* Strand ....1, D
Hunt street ....23, A
Hunter street, Brunswick square............11, A B
    " *"* Old Kent road ....28, B; 31, A
    " *"* Little, do...........................31, A
Huntingdon street ....18, C; 19, A; 20, A
Huntley street ....6, D
Hutchison street ....22, C
Hyde park ....2, D; 3, B; 7, C; 9, A
    " corner ....2, C; 3, A
    " gardens ....9, A
    " gate ....3, C
    " square ....7, D; 8, A; 9, A
    " street ....7, D; 9, A
    " place, Vincent square.....................4, C
    " road....................................17, B
    " street, Bloomsbury ....6, C
    " *"* Deptford ....30, D; 32, C
Hyde's place, Canonbury square....................16, D
Hyndman's grove ....32, A
    " street...............................32, B

Idol lane...22, B
Inverness place, Bayswater ....9, D
    " road, do. ....9, D
    " terrace, do. ....9, D
Ion square..20, A
Irongate Wharfs....................................8, A; 9, B
Ironmonger lane ....15, B; 18, A; 22, B
    " row, St. Luke's ....15, D
    " street......................................15, D
Isabella street ....27, C
Island row, Commercial road, East ......25, D; 26, B
Isle of Dogs ....26, A; 29, A
Islington green ....16, B; 17, A
Ivy lane, Hoxton ....19, A
    " Newgate street ....1, B; 6, A; 22, B
    " street, New ....19, A
    " *"* Old ....17, B; 19, A

Jacob street ....28, C
Jamaica place, Limehouse ....26, B
    " row, Bermondsey ....28, D; 31, C
    " street ....23, D; 25, C
James' place, Shacklewell ....19, C
    " *"* Stepney causeway....................25, D
    " *"* Walworth ....34, C

James' street, Ashley crescent .... Plate 15, D
    " *"* Bethnal-green ....20, B
    " *"* Bedford row ....6, D; 10, C
    " *"* Little, do. ....6, D; 10, C
    " *"* Birdcage walk ....20, A
    " *"* Buckingham Palace... 2, C; 4, B; 5, B
    " *"* Camberwell, New road ....33, C
    " *"* Camden road ....14, C
    " *"* *"* town ....13, D
    " *"* Cannon street road............ 22, C; 25, A
    " *"* Covent garden ....2, B; 6, C
    " *"* Green street, Bethnal-green ......20, D
    " *"* Goswell road............................15, C
    " *"* Haggerstone ....19, A
    " *"* Haymarket ....2, B
    " *"* Hoxton ....19, A
    " *"* Kensington square....................3, D
    " *"* Lambeth walk ....35, B
    " *"* Leonard street, Curtain road......18, C
    " *"* Limehouse ....23, D; 25, C D
    " *"* Great, Lisson grove ....8, B
    " *"* Maiden lane, Battle bridge.........14, A
    " *"* Margaret st., Hackney fds., 19, B; 21, A
    " *"* Marlborough road, Chelsea ....5, D
    " *"* Old street road ....15, D
    " *"* Oxford street ....7, C
    " *"* St. Peter's street, Islington ....17, A
    " *"* Walworth road................33, A ; 34, A
    " *"* Waterloo road ....27, C
    " *"* Westbourne terrace ....9, D
Jane street, Blackfriars road ....27, D
    " Commercial rd. East, 22, C; 23, B; 25, A
Jeffrey's street ....13, D
Jeremiah street ....26, A
Jermyn street ....1, D; 2, B
Jewin crescent ....15, A
    " street ....10, B; 15, A
Jewry street ....22, C
Jockeys fields...6, D
Johanna street ....27, C
John street, Adelphi ....1, D; 27, D
    " Albany road, Camberwell ....34, D
    " Back road, Kingsland ....19, C
    " Bedford row ....6, B D; 10, A C
    " *"* square, East ....23, B
    " Berkeley square ....2, D
    " Blackfriars road ....27, A
    " Bonner st., Bethnal-green, 20, D; 24, A
    " Cambridge heath ....20, C; 21, A
    " *"* road ....23, A
    " Cannon street road .... 22, C; 25, A
    " Chicksand street ....23, B
    " Church lane, Whitechapel... 22, C; 23, B
    " *"* road, Shadwell ....25, A
    " Commercial road, East ......23, D; 25, C
    " Cornwall road ....27, D
    " Curtain road ....18, C
    " East street, Walworth ....31, B; 34, C
    " Goldsmith's row ....20, A; 21, A
    " Great Suffolk street ....27, A
    " Harper street ....31, A
    " Hickman's folly ....28, D
    " Holland street, Blackfriars ....27, B
    " Horselydown ....28, A
    " Kingsland road..........................19, A
    " Leonard street, Finsbury ....18, C
    " Liverpool road ....14, B; 16, A
    " London field ....21, A
    " Marlborough road, Chelsea............5, D
    " Minories ....22, D
    " Old Kent road ....31, A B
    " Oxford street ....7, C
    " Pentonville ....10, D; 14, B
    " Poplar ....26, A
    " Portland street, Walworth, 34, A B
    " Regent street, Lambeth walk ......35, A
    " Regent's park ....12, B
    " Rhodeswell road ....23, D
    " Roupell street ....27, D

John street, Salmon's lane............ Plate 23, D; 25, D
"   "   Shacklewell lane .... 19, C
"   "   Spitalfields .... 18, D
"   "   Tottenham court road .... 6, D; 7, B
"   "   Waterloo road .... 27, D
"   "   White-horse lane, Stepney............. 23, C
"   "   White's row, Whitechapel .... 23, A
"   "   Lower, Commercial rd. East, 23, B ; 25, A
"   "   North, Poplar .... 26, A
"   "   West, Edgeware road .... 8, A
"   "   "   Hemingford road................ 14, B
"   "   Upper, Commercial rd. East, 23, B; 25, C
"   "   "   Hoxton.................. 18, C; 19, A
"   "   "   Tottenham court road.......... 7, B
John's hill .... 25, A
"   place, Islington .... 16, A
"   "   Bedford square, East .... 23, B
"   row, St. Luke's............................... 15, C D
Johnson street, Clarendon square .... 11, B; 13, A
"   "   Mile-end road .... 23, C
"   "   Millbank................................. 4, A
"   "   New road, St. George's, East, 25, A B
"   "   Old Gravel lane ,..................... 25, B
"   "   Sun Tavern fields .... 25, C
Joiner street, Lambeth road .... 33, B; 35, A
"   "   Tooley street .... 27, B; 28, A
Joiner's hall buildings, Upper Thames street.... 22, B
Jonathan street .... 35, D
Jubilee place, Chelsea .... 5, C D
"   "   Commercial road, East ....23, B ; 25, C
"   street .... 23, A B
Judd street .... 11, B
Juniper row, King David lane .... 25, B
Jurston street .... 27, C; 35, A

Keat street .... 18, B; 22, C
Kender street .... 32, D
Kennington common .... 33, D; 35, C
"   cross... 35, C
"   green .... 33, D; 35, C
"   lane, Lower...... 33, B D; 34, A; 35, A B
"   "   Upper .... 35, C
"   oval .... 35, C
"   place, Kennington green .... 33, D; 35, C
"   road, Clapham road......... 33, D; 34, A
"   "   Kennington cross....... 27, C; 35, A
"   row, Kennington common .... 35, C
Kensington gardens .... 3, D; 9, C
"   gate .... 3, D
"   gore .... 3, D
"   green .... 3, A
"   High street .... 3, D
"   square .... 3, D
"   street .... 4, C
Kent street, Borough .... 27, A; 28, B; 31, A
"   "   Haggerstone .... 19, B
"   terrace, Park road, Regent's park........... 12, A
Kentish-town road .... 13, D
Kenton road .... 21, D; 24, C
"   street .... 11, A
Keppel street, Chelsea .... 3, C ; 5, D
"   "   Russell square........................... 6, D
Kilburn gate .... 8, D; 12, D
Kildare grove... 9, D
Kinder street.. 23, B
King square... 15, C
"   street, Bartholomew square .... 15, D
"   "   Bermondsey New road .... 31, A
"   "   Borough .... 27, A; 28, A
"   "   Borough road......... 27, A; 33, B; 35, A
"   "   Cambridge road.......................... 23, A
"   "   Camden-town .... 13, B D
"   "   Cheapside .... 15, B; 18, A; 22, B
"   "   Chelsea .... 5, D
"   "   Clerkenwell .... 15, C
"   "   Commercial rd. East 22, C; 23, B; 25, A
"   "   Covent garden..................... 1, D; 6, C
"   "   Drury lane .... 6, C
"   "   East street, Walworth....... 33, A; 34, A

King street, Finsbury............................. Plate 18, C
"   "   Golden square .... 7, A
"   "   Green street, Stepney .... 23, D
"   "   Grosvenor square......................... 7, C
"   "   Hackney road .... 20, A
"   "   Holborn .... 6, D
"   "   Kensington .... 3, D
"   "   Kingsland .... 19, A
"   "   Lambeth walk .... 35, A B
"   "   Long acre .... 2, B; 6, C
"   "   Mile-end, New-town................... 23, A
"   "   New North road .... 16, B; 17, C
"   "   Old Ford road................... 20, C; 24, A
"   "   Old Kent road................ 31, D; 34, C
"   "   Poplar .... 26, A
"   "   Portman square .... 7, D
"   "   Rotherhithe .... 28, D
"   "   St. James' square .... 2, B
"   "   Snowhill .... 6, A; 10, B; 15, A
"   "   Soho .... 2, B; 6, C; 7, A
"   "   Spitalfields .... 18, D; 20, B
"   "   Tower hill................................... 22, D
"   "   Turk street, Bethnal-green .... 20, B
"   "   Upper Ebury street .... 5, A
"   "   Wapping .... 35, B
"   "   Westminster .... 2, A; 4, A
"   "   Little, Camden-town .... 13, C D
"   "   New, Deptford .... 30, C
"   "   Upper, Old Kent road .... 31, D; 34, C
"   "   Mews .... 7, C; 9, A
King David fort.. 25, A
"   "   lane .... 25, B
"   Edward street, Lambeth road,................. 35, A
"   "   "   Liverpool road .... 16, A
"   "   "   Mile-end, New-town.......23, B
"   "   "   Newgate street, 6, A; 10, B; 15, A
"   Edward's road .... 21, B; 24, C
"   Henry's walk .... 17, C
"   William street, City .... 18, B; 22, B
"   "   "   Strand.............................. 1, D
King's cross .... 10, C; 11, B; 13, B; 14, A
"   road, Asylum road .... 32, B
"   "   Ball's pond road .... 19, C
"   "   Chelsea .... 5, C D
"   "   Gray's Inn lane .... 6, B D; 10, A
"   "   Homerton .... 21, D; 24, D
"   "   Kingsland road .... 19, A
"   "   St. Pancras .... 13, B; 14, A C
King's row, Horselydown............................. 28, A
"   "   Walworth road............. 33, C ; 34, B
Kingsgate street .... 6, D
Kingsland crescent... 19, A
"   green .... 17, D; 19, C
"   road ....17, D; 18, C D; 19, A C; 20, A B
Kinnerton street .... 2, C; 3, A
Kirby street .... 10, A
Kirk's row, Rhodeswell road .... 23, D
Knightrider street .... 1, A; 22, B
Knightsbridge.. 3, A B
Knotsford street .... 20, D; 24, A

Labour-in-vain street .... 25, D
Lady Lake's grove....................................... 23, A
Lamb alley, Bermondsey street............. 28, B; 31, A
"   lane .... 21, B
"   street .... 18, D
Lamb's buildings, Chiswell street .... 15, B
"   passage,   do.   .... 15, B
"   Conduit street .... 6, D; 10, A C
Lambeth hill .... 1, A; 22, B
"   road .... 27, A C; 33, B; 35, A
"   square .... 35, B
"   street .... 22, C; 23, B; 25, A
"   walk .... 35, A B
Lancelot place, Brompton road .... 3, A
Langdale street .... 22, C; 25, A
Langford place, Abbey road .... 12, C D
Langham place, Regent street .... 7, B
Langley street .... 2, B; 6, C

Lansdowne place, Brunswick square, Plate 6, D; **11, A**
   " road...............................19, B D; 21, A
   " street.................................27, A; 31, A
Lant place, Southwark Bridge road......27, A; 31, A
   " street.................................27, A; 31, A
Lark row, Cambridge heath..................20, C; 21, B
Laundry yard, Westminster.............................4, A
Laura place, Clapton.................................21, D
Laurel street.......................................19, C D
Laurie place, New cross.............................32, D
Lausanne road......................................32, D
Lavender grove......................................21, A
   " lane...29, A
   " place, Bayswater...............................9, C
   " " Rotherhithe.......................29, A
Lavina grove, Caledonian road......................14, A
Lawn, The, South Lambeth............................35, D
Lawrence lane.....................15, A; 18, A; 22, B
   " street..5, C
   " Pountney lane...............................22, B
   " " hill.....................................22, B
Lawson street......................................31, A
Laxon street...........................27, A; 28, B; 31, A
Laystall street....................................10, A C
Leadenhall market..................................22, B
   " street.....................................22, A B C
Leader street.......................................5, D
Leading street.....................................25, B
Leather lane....................................6, B; 10, A
Lebanon place, Walworth.............................34, C
Lee street...19, A
Lee's mews...7, C
Leicester place, Leicester square...................6, C
   " square.................................1, D; 2, B
Leigh street.......................................11, B
Leinster terrace, Cleveland square..................9, D
Leipsic road.......................................33, C
Leman street.........................22, C; 23, B; 25, A
Lemon street.......................................27, A
Leonard place, Circus road.........................12, C
   " street, Finsbury.............15, D; 18, C
   " " Vauxhall Bridge road.............4, D
Lewis street.......................................13, D
Lewisham road......................................32, D
Leybourne road.....................................13, D
Lichfield street................................2, B; 6, C
Lillington street..............................4, C D
Lime street..22, B
Limehouse causeway.................................26, B
   " cut.........................23, D; 26, B
Limekiln hill......................................26, B
Lincoln street, Bow road...........................24, B
   " " King's road, Chelsea................5, D
Lincoln's Inn.......................................6, A
   " " fields......................................6, C
Linden grove..9, C
Linton street...................................17, A B
Lion street....................................31, B; 33, A
Liquorpond street..................................10, A
Lisbon street......................................23, A
Lisle street....................................2, B; 6, C
Lisson grove..8, B
   " street..8, A
   " " Upper....................................8, A
Little Britain...................6, A; 10, B; 15, A
   " Moorfields...............................15, B; 18, A
Livermore road.................................19, A B
Liverpool road...............14, D; 15, C; 16, A C
   " street, Bishopsgate..............18, B; 22, A
   " " King's cross..............10, C; 11, B
   " " Walworth.............33, C; 34, A
Lloyd place, Brompton road...........................3, A
   " square...10, C
   " street...10, C
Lloyd's row, St. John street road..................10, D
Lodge place, St. John's wood..................8, B; 12, A
   " road, do. ....8, B; 12, A
Loman street.......................................27, A
Lombard street, Chelsea.............................5, C
   " " City.....................................22, B

Lombard street, Southwark...................Plate 27, A
London bridge.......................22, B; 27, B; 28, A
   " field.............................19, D; 21, A
   " lane...21, A B
   " road.....................27, A; 31, B; 33, B; 35, A
   " street, Great Western Railway....8, A; 9, B
   " " London road.................31, A; 33, B
   " " Ratcliff....................................25, D
   " " Tottenham court road...............7, B
   " " Up. North st. Whitechapel, 20,B; 23,A
   " " William st. Caledo. road, 13, B; 14, A
   " terrace, London field................19, D; 21, A
   " wall.............................15, B; 18, A
Long acre.......................................2, B; 6, C
   " alley, Sun street, Bishopsgate.............18, B D
   " lane, Bermondsey.............27, A; 28, B; 31 A
   " " West Smithfield.................10, B; 15, A
   " yard, Lamb's Conduit street..................10, C
Lonsdale square....................................16, A
Lorimore road..................................33, C; 34, B
   " terrace, do. ....33, C; 34, A
Lothbury......................................15, B; 18, A
Loudoun road.......................................12, C D
Loughborough street................................35, C
Louisa street......................................23, C
Love lane, Bankside............................1, A; 27, B
   " " Eastcheap...............................22, B
   " " Rotherhithe............................28, D
   " " Shadwell...............................25, D
   " " Wood street, City..............15, B; 18, A
Lovegrove street.....................31, D; 32, A; 34, C D
Lower road, Islington..............................17, C
   " street, do. ....16, B; 17, A C
   " " Shadwell...............................25, B D
   " marsh, Lambeth.....................27, C; 35, B
Lowndes place, Belgrave square......................5, B
   " square..3, A
   " street............................3, A; 5, B
Lowther grove, Holloway road.............14, D; 16, C
Luard street.......................................14, B
Lucas road...33, D
   " street, Commercial road, East......23, B; 25, C
   " " Rotherhithe.........................28, D
Ludgate hill......................1, B; 6, A; 10, A; 15, A
   " street...........................10, B; 15, A
Luke street, Buxton street, Mile-end New town, 23, A
   " " Finsbury...........................18, C
   " " North street, Whitechapel...........23, A
Lupus street...................................4, C D
Lyall street..5, B
Lyon mews..8, B
   " street..14, D

Mabledon place, Burton crescent....................11, B
Macclesfield street, City road..............15, C; 17, A
   " " Soho...............................6, C
Maddox street.......................................7, A
Madras place, Holloway road.................14, D; 16, C
Magdalen place, Great Prescott street...............25, A
   " street.....................................28, A
Maida hill..8, B
   " " West....................................8, A C
Maiden lane, Battle bridge.........................14, C
   " " Covent garden...........................1, D
   " " Queen street, Cheapside...........22, B
Maidstone street.........................20, A; 21, A
Mail-coach yard, Kingsland road.....................20, A
Maismore square.........................32, B; 34, D
Mall, The, Notting hill.............................9, C
   " " St. James' park..........................2, A
Maltby street......................................28, B
Malvern road.................................19, B D; 21, A
   " terrace, Thornhill road............14, B; 16, A
Manchester square..................................7, D
   " street, Gray's Inn road......10, C; 11, B
   " " Manchester square..............7, D
   " " Waterloo-town.................20, B
   " " Great do. ....20, B; 23, A
Manley place, Kennington common.................33, D

Manners street .... Plate 27, D
Manning street .... 28, B; 31, A
Manor grove, Hatcham New town .... 32, A
  "   place, Haggerstone .... 19, B
  "   "   Paddington green .... 8, A
  "   "   Walworth road .... 33 C; 34, A
  "   road, Bermondsey .... 30, B; 31, C; 32. A
  "   "   Walworth .... 33, C; 34, A B
  "   "   Well street, Hackney .... 21, B; 24, C
  "   street, Chelsea .... 5, C
  "   "   Upper, do. .... 5, C
  "   "   Old Kent road .... 32, A B
Mansell street .... 22, C
Mansfield street, Borough road .... 33, B; 35, A
  "   "   Kingsland road .... 19, A
  "   "   Portland place .... 7, B
Mansion-house street .... 33, D; 35, A
Map's row .... 23, C
Mape street .... 20, B; 23, A
Marchmont street .... 11, A
Mare street .... 21, A B; 24, C
Margaret row, Hackney fields .... 19, B; 21, A
  "   place,   do. .... 20, C; 21, A
  "   street, Cavendish square .... 7, A
  "   "   Commercial road, East, 23, D; 25, D
  "   "   Hackney fields, 19, B; 20, A; 21, A
  "   "   Well street, Hackney, 21, D; 24, C
  "   "   Wilmington square .... 10, C
Margaretta terrace, Chelsea .... 5, C
Maria street, Beaumont square .... 23, C
  "   "   Kingsland road .... .18, D; 19, A; 20, A
  "   "   West Ferry road .... 26, D
  "   terrace, Barnsbury square .... 14, B
  "   "   Hill street, Peckham .... 34, D
Marian square .... 20, C; 21, A
Marigold street .... 28, D
Marine street .... 28, D
Mark lane .... 22, D
  "   street .... 18, C
Market hill .... 25, B
  "   street, Borough road .... 31, A; 33, B
  "   "   Edgeware road .... 8, A; 9, B
  "   "   Finsbury market .... 18, D
  "   "   London road .... 33, B
  "   "   Millbank .... 4, A
  "   "   Poplar .... 26, A
  "   "   St. John street road .... 15, C
  "   "   Stepney .... 23, C D
Markham square .... 5, C
  "   street .... 5, D
Marlborough hill, St. John's wood .... 12, D
  "   place,   do. .... 8, D; 12, C
  "   road, Chelsea .... 3, C; 5, D
  "   "   Dalston .... 19, B
  "   "   Old Kent road, 31, D; 32, A; 34, C
  "   "   St. John's wood .... 12, D
  "   square .... 5, D
  "   street, Blackfriars road .... 27, A
  "   "   Great, Oxford street .... 7, A
Marquis road .... 17, C
Marsh lane, Battersea .... 36, D
Marshall street, Golden square .... 7, A
  "   "   London road .... 33, B
Marsham street .... 4, A
Martha street, Cambridge heath .... 20, C; 21, A
  "   "   Church road, Shadwell .... 25, A
  "   "   Haggerstone .... 19, B
Martin street .... 15, D
Martin's lane .... 22, B
Mary street, Arlington square .... 17, A
  "   "   Hampstead road .... 11, C D
  "   "   Kingsland road .. .. 19, A
  "   "   Lambeth .... 27. C; 35, B
  "   "   Ocean street, Stepney .... 23, C
  "   "   Poplar .... 26, A
  "   "   Rhodeswell road .... 23, D
  "   "   Upper Chapman street .... 25, A
Marylebone lane .... 7, D
  "   street .... 2, B

Marylebone street, Great .... Plate 7, B
  "   "   Little .... 7, B
  "   "   Upper .... 7, B
Mason street, Grove street, Deptford .... 29, D
  "   "   Old Kent road .... 31, B; 34, C
  "   "   New cross .... 32, D
  "   "   Westminster bridge road, 27, C; 35, B
Mawbey road .... 31, D; 34, C
Mayfield road, Dalston .... 19, A C
  "   street, do. .... 17, D; 19, C
  "   terrace, do. .... 19, C
Maze, The, Tooley street .... 28, A
  "   Pond .... 27, A; 28, A
  "   "   Great .... 27, A; 28, A
Mead row, Westminster road .... 27, C; 35, A
Meadow row, New Kent road .... 31, B; 33, A
  "   road .... 35, C
Meard's street .... 7, A
Mecklenburgh square .... 10, C
Medburn street .... 13, B
Medes place, Newington causeway .... 31, A; 33, B
Medway street .... 4, A
Meeting-house alley, Wapping .... 25, B
Melcombe place, Dorset square .... 8, B
Melina place, Grove-end road .... 8, D; 12, C
Melior street .... 28, A
Mellish street .... 26, D
Melton street .... 11, B
Mercer street .... 2, B; 6, C
Mercers' row, Shadwell .... 25, B
Meredith street .... 10, D
Mermaid court, Borough .... 27, A
Merrow street .... 33, C; 34, B
Merton road .... 3, C
Michael's grove, Brompton .... 3, C
  "   place,   do. .... 3, C
Middle row, Holborn .... 6, A; 10, A
  "   Temple lane .... 1, B; 6, A
Middlesex street, Somers-town .... 11, B; 13, A
  "   "   Whitechapel .... 18, B; 22, A C
Middleton road .... 19, A B
Midway place, Deptford Lower road .... 30, A
Mildmay road .... 19, C
Mile-end road .... 23, C; 24, A
Miles street .... 35, D
Milford grove .... 32, B
  "   lane .... 1, B; 6, A
Milk street .... 15, A; 18, A; 22, B
  "   yard, New Gravel lane .... 25, B
Mill lane, Bermondsey .... 31, C
  "   "   Tooley street .... 28, A
  "   place, Commercial road, East ...... 23, D; 25, D
  "   street, Dockhead .... 28, A B
  "   "   Hanover square .... 7, A
  "   "   Lambeth walk .... 35, B
  "   yard, Wellclose square .... 25, A
Millbank road .... 4, C
  "   row .... 4, A C
  "   street .... 4, A
Millman street .... 6, D; 10, C
  "   "   New .... 6, D
Mill-pond row, Bermondsey .... 28, D
  "   "   street .... 28, D
Milner square .... 16, A
  "   street, Marlborough road, Chelsea, 3, A; 5, D
  "   "   Milner square .... 16, A
Milton street, Cripplegate .... 15, B
  "   "   Dorset square .... 8, B
Mina road .... 31, D; 34, C
Mincing lane .... 22, B
Minera street .... 5, B
Minerva street .... 20, C
Minories .... 22, C D
Mint street .... 27, A; 31, A
Mintern street .... 15, D; 17, B
Minto street .... 28, B; 31, A
Mistear's buildings, Rotherhithe .... 29, A
Mitcham street .... 8, A B
Mitchell street, Great .... 15, C D

26

Mitre street, Aldgate .... Plate 22, C
    "   "   New cut .... 27, C
Moiety road .... 26, D
Moira place, Victoria road, Kensington .... 3, D
Molyneux street .... 8, A
Moneyer street .... 15, D
Monkwell street .... 10, B ; 15, A
Monmouth road .... 9, D
Montague close .... 27, B
    "   place, Montague square .... 7, D ; 8, B
    "   "   Russell square .... 6, D
    "   row, Islington .... 17, A
    "   square .... 7, D ; 8, B
    "   street, Borough road .... 27, A ; 31, A
    "   "   Gossett street .... 20, B
    "   "   Montague square .... 7, D
    "   "   Upper, do. .... 7, D ; 8, B
    "   "   Russell square .... 6, D
    "   "   Spitalfields .... 18, D ; 23, A
    "   "   Old, Whitechapel .... 23, B
Montford place, Kennington-green .... 35, C
Montpelier lane .... 33, C ; 34, B
    "   place, Montpelier square .... 3, A
    "   row,   do.   .... 3, A
    "   square .... 3, A B
    "   street .... 34, B
Monument yard .... 22, B
Moon street .... 16, A
Moor lane .... 15, B
    "   street .... 6, C ; 7, A
Moore street .... 3, A ; 5, D
    "   terrace, Maismore square .... 32, B ; 34, D
Moorgate street .... 15, B
Moreton place, Pimlico .... 4, D
    "   street, Newington causeway .... 31, B ; 33, B
    "   "   Pimlico .... 4, C
    "   terrace, do.   .... 4, D
Morgan lane .... 28, A
    "   street, Commercial road, East, 22, C ; 23, B ; 25, A
    "   "   Tredegar square .... 24, A B
Morning lane .... 21, D
Mornington crescent .... 11, D ; 13, A
    "   road .... 11, D ; 13, A C
    "   street .... 13, C
Morpeth road .... 24, C
    "   street .... 20, D ; 24, A
    "   terrace, Victoria park .... 20, C ; 21, B
Mortimer market .... 7, B ; 11, A
    "   road .... 17, D ; 19, A
    "   street .... 7, B
Morton place, Lambeth road .... 35, A
Moscow road .... 9, D
Motcomb street .... 3, A
Motley street .... 18, C D
Mott's lane .... 17, C
Mount gardens, Mount street, Lambeth, 27, C ; 35, B
    "   pleasant .... 10, C
    "   row,   Berkeley square .... 2, D ; 7, C
    "   street,   do.   .... 2, D ; 7, C
    "   "   Bethnal-green .... 18, D ; 20, B
    "   "   Lambeth .... 27, C ; 35, B
    "   "   Walworth road .... 33, C ; 34, B
    "   "   Whitechapel .... 23, B
Mountford street .... 23, B
Mulberry street .... 22, C ; 23, B
Munster square .... 11, C
    "   street .... 11, C D
Murray street, Camden square .... 14, C
    "   "   New North road .... 15, D
Museum street .... 6, C D
Myddelton place, St. John street road .... 15, C
    "   row,   do.   .... 10, D
    "   square .... 10, D
    "   street .... 10, D
Mylne street .... 10, D
Myrtle street, Dalston .... 19, A
    "   "   Hoxton .... 18, C

Napier street, Ashley crescent .... 17, B

Napier street, Great Dover street, Plate 27, A ; 31, A
    "   terrace, Islington .... 16, A
Narrow street .... 25, D
Nassau street, Middlesex hospital .... 7, B
    "   "   Soho .... 2, B ; 6, C
Navarino grove, Dalston .... 19, D ; 21, C
    "   place,   do.   .... 19, D ; 21, C
Neate street .... 34, D
Neckinger road .... 28, B D ; 31, C
    "   street .... 28, B
Nelson place, St. James' road .... 31, C
    "   "   Walworth .... 34, A
    "   square .... 27, A
    "   street, Boundary st. Shoreditch, 18, D ; 20, B
    "   "   Camberwell .... 33, C
    "   "   City road .... 15, D
    "   "   Hackney road .... 20, A
    "   "   Long lane, Bermondsey, 27, A ; 28, B ; 31, A
    "   "   Margaret st. Hackney fields, 19, B ; 21, A
    "   "   New rd. Commercial rd. East, 23, B; 25, A
    "   "   Stepney .... 23, C
    "   "   Walworth .... 31, B ; 33, A
    "   terrace, City road .... 15, C
Neptune street, Rotherhithe .... 28, D ; 30, A
    "   "   Wandsworth road .... 35, D ; 36, A
    "   "   Walworth .... 31, B ; 33, A ; 34, A
Neville street .... 35, C
New cut, Homerton .... 21, D
    "   Lambeth .... 27, C
    "   inn .... 1, B ; 6, C
    "   river .... 10, D ; 15, C ; 16, D ; 17, C
    "   road, Battersea fields .... 36, A
    "   "   Regent's park ..... 7, B ; 8, A B ; 11, A B C
    "   "   St. George's, East .... 22, C ; 25, A
    "   "   Sloane street, Chelsea ...... 3, A ; 5, B D
    "   "   Whitechapel road .... 23, B ; 25, A
    "   row, Rotherhithe .... 28, D ; 30, A
    "   square, Horselydown .... 28, A
    "   "   Lincoln's inn .... 6, A
    "   street, Backchurch lane, Whitechapel, 22. C ; 25, A
    "   "   Bermondsey .... 28, B ; 31, C
    "   "   Bishopsgate .... 18, B ; 22, A
    "   "   Borough road .... 33, B ; 35, A
    "   "   Brompton .... 3, A
    "   "   City road .... 15, D
    "   "   Covent garden .... 1, D ; 2 B
    "   "   Dockhead .... 28, A
    "   "   Dorset square .... 8, B
    "   "   East street, Lambeth walk .... 35, A
    "   "   "   Walworth, 31, B; 33, A; 34, A
    "   "   Edward street, Kingsland road ...... 18, C
    "   "   Fieldgate street, Whitechapel ...... 23, B
    "   "   Golden square .... 7, A
    "   "   Kennington road .... 33, D ; 34, A
    "   "   Limehouse .... 26, B
    "   "   Lower Shadwell .... 25, B
    "   "   New road, Whitechapel .... 23, B
    "   "   New Kent road .... 31, B ; 33, A
    "   "   Poplar .... 26, A
    "   "   Portland town .... 12, A
    "   "   Prince's road, Lambeth .... 35, C
    "   "   Rotherhithe .... 30, A
    "   "   St. Thomas' street, Borough, 27, B ; 28, A
    "   "   Southwark Bridge road .... 27, B
    "   "   Spring gardens .... 1, D
    "   "   Vincent square .... 4, A
    "   "   Virginia row .... 20, B
    "   "   Webber street, Blackfriars road ..... 27, C
    "   "   Great, Fetter lane .... 1, B ; 6, A
    "   "   Little, Shoe lane .... 1, B ; 6, A
New Bridge street, Blackfriars .... 1, B ; 6, A
    "   "   Vauxhall .... 35, D
    "   Buckenham square .... 31, A
    "   Church road, St. George's, Camberwell .... 34, B
    "   "   South Hackney .... 21, B ; 24, C
    "   "   street, Bermondsey .... 28, D
    "   Cross road .... 32, D
    "   Inn street .... 18, D
    "   "   yard .... 18, D ; 20, B

New Kent road .... Plate 31, B ; 33, A
    " North road .... 15, D ; 16, B D ; 17, B C
    " North street ....18, C
    " York street .... 20, D
Newberry place, Prince of Wales' road............ 13, D
Newcastle street.................................. 1, D ; 6, C
Newgate market.............. 1, B ; 6, A ; 10, B ; 15, A
    " street .... 1, B ; 6, A ; 10, B ; 15, A
Newhall street .... 17, C
Newington butts .... 33, B
    " causeway .... 27, A ; 31, A; 33, B
    " crescent .... 33, B; 34, A
    " green ....17, C
Newland street .... 5, B
Newman street .... 6, C ; 7, A
Newnham street....................................... 8, A
Newport market .... 2, B ; 6, C
    " street .... 2, B ; 6, C
    " " Little .... 2, B ; 6, C
Newton road .... 9, D
    " street....................................... 6, C
Nicholas lane... 22, B
    " street .... 15, D ; 17, B ; 18, C
Nichol's row, Church street, Shoreditch......... 20, B
    " street, Half ....18, D ; 20, B
    " " New ....18, D ; 20, B
    " " Old ....18, D ; 20, B
Nicholl's square, Aldersgate street................. 15, A
    " " Hackney road...............19, A ; 20, A
    " street, Margaret st. Hackney fds. 19, B; 20, A
Nightingale lane .... 22, D ; 25, A
Nile place, Weymouth street, New Kent road, 33, A
    " street .... 15, D; 18, C
Nine Elms .... 4, C ; 35, D ; 36, A
Noble street, Cheapside .... 6, A ; 15, A ; 18, A
    " " Goswell street .... 15, C
Noel street, Islington .... 15, C ; 17, A
    " " Wardour street, Soho .... 7, A
Norfolk crescent.................................. 8, A ; 9, B
    " place, Lambeth.............................. 35, B
    " road ....12, B
    " street, Cambridge road .... 23, A
    " " Globe road....................... 23, C
    " " Gt. Charlotte st. Blackfriars rd. 27, A
    " " Hyde road, Hoxton .... 17, B
    " " Islington .... 16, B : 17, C
    " " New, do........................... 17, C
    " " King's cross .... 13, B
    " " Middlesex hospital .... 7, B
    " " New road, Whitechapel, 23, B ; 25, A
    " " Park lane..................... 7, C ; 9, A
    " " Southwark Bridge road.............. 27, A
    " " Strand .... 1, B
    " " Upper Kennington lane .... 35, C
North bank, St. John's wood .... 8, B ; 12, A
    " crescent, Bedford square .... 6, D ; 7, B
    " place, Cromer street .... 11, B
    " " Globe street, Bethnal-green .... 20, D
    " row, Park lane....................... 7, C ; 9, A
    " street, Back Church lane... 22, C ; 23, B ; 25, A
    " " Cambridge heath .... 20, C ; 21, A
    " " Edgeware road .... 8, B
    " " Finsbury market .... 18, D
    " " Globe road .... 20, D
    " " John street, Fitzroy square .... 7, B
    " " Lambeth .... 35, A
    " " Manchester square ....a....... 7, D
    " " Pentonville..................10, C ; 14, A B
    " " Upper, do. .... 13, B ; 14, A
    " " Poplar .... 26, A
    " " Upper, do. .... 26, A
    " " Red Lion square .... 6, D
    " " Sidney st. Commercial road, East, 23, A
    " " Sloane street, Chelsea .... 3, A
    " " Stepney............................ 23, D
    " " Walworth .... 31, B; 34, A
    " " Whitechapel road .... 23, A
    " " Little, do................................ 23, A
    " " Upper, do.................. 20, D ; 23, A

North terrace, Alexander square .... Plate 3, C
    " Audley street .... 7, C
    " Conduit street ....20, B
    " Wharf road, King's cross .... 13, B ; 14, A
    " " " Paddington................ 8, A ; 9, B
Northam's buildings, Somers-town .... 11, B
Northampton park .... 17, C
    " place, Walworth .... 31, B ; 34, A
    " road .... 10, D
    " square .... 15, C
    " street, Cambridge road .... 23, A
    " " Clerkenwell .... 15, C
    " " Little, do....................... 15, C
    " " Islington .... 16, B ; 17, C
    " " King's cross................... 13, B
    " " Old Kent road .... 31, D ; 34, C
Northumberland street, Marylebone .... 7, D
    " " Strand .... 1, D
Northwick terrace, St. John's wood road .... 8, B
Norton Folgate .... 18, D
    " street, Green st. Bethnal-green, 20, D ; 24, A
    " " Portland road .... 7, B
    " " Upper, do.................. 7, B ; 11, C
Nottingham place, Marylebone .... 11, C
    " " Whitechapel................23, B
    " street, Marylebone .... 7, B D
    " " Waterloo-town.............20, B
Nursery row, Walworth .... 31, B; 33, A ; 34, A
Nutford place, Edgeware road .... 8, A ; 9, B

Oak lane .... 25, D ; 26, B
    " tree road .... 8, B
Oakey street, Bethnal-green .... 20, B
Oakham street .... 5, D
Oakley square, Camden-town .... 13, A
    " " Chelsea .... 5, C
    " street, Chelsea .... 5, C
    " " Lambeth .... 27, C ; 35, A
Ocean street .... 23, C
Offord road .... 14, D
Ogle street, Upper .... 7, B
Old street .... 15, C D
    " " road .... 15, D ; 18, C ; 20, B
    " Bailey................. 1, B ; 6, A ; 10, B ; 15, A
    " Brompton .... 3, C
    " Change .... 6, A ; 15, A ; 22, B
    " Church road, Stepney .... 23, D
    " Fish street .... 1, A ; 18, A ; 22, B
    " " hill...................... 1, A ; 22, B
    " Ford road................... 20, C D ; 24, A B
    " Jewry .... 15, B ; 18, A ; 22, B
    " Kent road .... 31, B D ; 32, B ; 34, C
    " Manor road, Stepney .... 23, D
Omega terrace, Alpha road............................ 8, B
Onslow crescent .... 3, C
    " square............................. 3, C ; 5, D
Orange street, Bethnal-green .... 20, B
    " " Gravel lane, Southwark .... 27, A
    " " Leicester square................... 2, B
Orchard grove, Lower road, Islington .... 17, C
    " street, Hackney .... 21, B ; 24, C
    " " Kentish-town .... 13, D
    " " Portman square .... 7, C
    " " St. Luke's .... 15, D
    " " Wandsworth road .... 35, D ; 36, A
    " " Westminster................... 4, A
Ord street.. 26, D
Ordnance road .... 12, B
Orford street .... 5, D
Orme square .... 9, C
Ormesby street .... 19, A
Ormond street .... 6, D
    " " Great .... 6, D ; 11, A
    " " New .... 10, C
Orsett place, Westbourne terrace................... 9, D
    " street .... 35, C
    " terrace, Orsett place........................ 9, D
Osborne place, Osborne street, Whitechapel .... 23, B
    " street, Walworth .... 34, A

Osborne street, Whitechapel .... Plate 22, C ; 23, B
Osnaburgh street... 11, C
    "   terrace, Osnaburgh street .... 11, C
Ossory road... 31, D ; 34, D
Ossulston street .... 11, B ; 13, A
Otto street... 33, D
Oval, The, Hackney road .... 20, C ; 21, A
    "   Kennington.. 35, C
    "   road, Kennington.................................... 35, C
    "   *"* Regent's park.................................... 13, C
Ovington square .... 3, A
Owen street, Goswell road .... 10, D ; 15, C
Owen's row,   do.   .... 10, D ; 15, C
Oxendon street .... 1, D ; 2, B
Oxford crescent, St. Pancras........................ 13, B
    "   market.. 7, A
    "   road, Islington .... 17, C
    "   *"* St. Pancras .... 13, B
    "   square.. 8, A ; 9, B
    "   street .... 6, C ; 7, A C ; 9, A
    "   *"* Islington .... 17, C
    "   *"* London hospital......................... 23, B
    "   *"* Lower, do............................... 23, B
    "   *"* St. Pancras .... 13, B
    "   terrace, Edgeware road .... 8, A ; 9, B

Paddington canal .... 8, C
    "   green .... 8, A ; 9, B
    "   street .... 7, D
Page street .... 4, C
Page's walk .... 31, C
Pakenham street .... 10, C
Palace road .... 27, C ; 35, B
    "   street... 4, B
    "   yard, New .... 4, A
    "   *"* Old .... 4, A
Palestine place, Cambridge road.................... 20, C
Pall mall .... 1, D ; 2, B
    "   *"* East .... 2, B
Palmer place, Holloway .... 14, D ; 16, C
    "   street,   do.   .... 14, D ; 16, C
    "   *"* Stepney .... 23, D
Pancras lane .... 15, A ; 18, A ; 22, B
    "   road .... 10, C ; 11, B ; 13, B
    "   street .... 6, D ; 7, B
Panton square .... 2 ,B
    "   street .... 1, D ; 2, B
Parade, Lambeth .... 35, B
Paradise place, Hackney .... 21, D
    "   row, Bethnal-green......................... 20, D
    "   *"* Hackney .... 21, D
    "   *"* Islington.................. 16, B ; 17, A
    "   *"* Rotherhithe .... 28, D ; 30, A
    "   street, Finsbury .... 15, B ; 18, C
    "   *"* King's cross.............................. 10, C
    "   *"* Lambeth .... 35, B
    "   *"* Marylebone .... 7, D
    "   *"* Rotherhithe.............................. 28, D
    "   walk, Queen's road, Chelsea .... 5, C
Paragon, New Kent road................................. 31, B
    "   row, Walworth .... 31, B
Paris street .... 35, B
    "   Little .... 27, C ; 35, B
Parish street .... 28, A
Park crescent, Regent's park.................... 7, B ; 11, C
Park lane, Hyde park .... 2, D ; 7, C ; 9, A
    "   *"* Kensington.............................. 3, C D
    "   *"* Liverpool road .... 14, D ; 16, C
    "   place, Commercial road, Old Kent road ... 32, B
    "   *"* Knightsbridge .... 3, B
    "   *"* Lambeth .... 35, B
    "   *"* Paddington green .... 8, A
    "   *"* St. James' street .... 2, B
    "   *"* Walworth .... 31, B ; 34, A
    "   *"* Upper, Regent's park, 8, B ; 11, C ; 12, A
    "   road, Dalston .... 19, D ; 21, C
    "   *"* Islington.......................... 14, B ; 16, A
    "   *"* New cross .... 32, D
    "   *"* Old ford .... 24, B

Park road, Old Kent road, Plate 31, D ; 32, B ; 34, D
    "   *"* Lower, do.   .... 32, B ; 34, D
    "   *"* Regent's park....................8, B ; 12, A
    "   *"* terrace, Battersea .... 36, D
    " square .... 11, C
    " street, Bethnal-green........................... 20, D
    "   *"* Camberwell .... 34, B
    "   *"* Cambridge road .... 23, A
    "   *"* Camden-town .... 13, D
    "   *"* Dorset square .... 8, B ; 11, C ; 12, A
    "   *"* East road, City road .... 15, D ; 18, C
    "   *"* Grosvenor square........ 2, D ; 7, C ; 9, A
    "   *"* Hackney wick .... 24, D
    "   *"* Highbury .... 16, D.
    "   *"* Islington .... 16, C
    "   *"* Upper, do................... 14, D ; 16, C
    "   *"* Kennington cross....................... 35, C
    "   *"* Limehouse................................. 26, B
    "   *"* Park road, Old Kent road... 32, B ; 34, D
    "   *"* Southwark .... 27, B
    "   *"* New, do............................ 1, A ; 27, B
    "   *"* Westminster .... 4, A
    " terrace, Battersea .... 36. D
    "   *"* Regent's park .... 12, A
    " village, East .... 11, D ; 13, C
    "   *"* West.. 13, C
Parker street, Drury lane .... 6, C
    "   *"* Kingsland road......................... 19, A
    "   *"* Westminster .... 4, A
Parker's buildings, Spa road .... 28, B ; 31, C
    "   row, Dockhead .... 28, D
Parkfield street .... 10, D ; 16, A ; 17, A
Parliament street, Cambridge road .... 20, D
    "   *"* Westminster ......1, C ; 2, A ; 4, A
Paternoster row .... 1, B ; 10, B ; 22, B
Patriot square .... 20, D
Patterson street .... 23, D
Paul street.. 18, C
Paul's chain............................... 6, A ; 15, A ; 22, B
Paulin street .... 28, B ; 31, C
Paulton square .... 5, C
Pavement, Finsbury .... 15, B ; 18, A
Payne street .... 14, B
Peacock street .... 33, B ; 34, A
Pearl row, Blackfriars road .... 27, A ; 33, B ; 35, A
    " street .... 18, D
Pearson street .... 19, A
Pear-tree street .... 15, C
Peckham lane .... 32, B
    " grove .... 34, D
Peerless row, City road.................................... 18, C
Pelham crescent .... 3, C ; 5, D
    " place .... 3, C ; 5, D
    " road .... 3, C ; 5, D
    " street .... 18, D ; 23, A
Pell street.. 22, C ; 25, A
Pembroke mews .... 2, C ; 3, A
Pembury grove .... 19, D ; 21, C
    " road .... 19, D ; 21, C
Pennington street .... 22, D ; 25, A
Pennyfields .... 26, A
Penton place, Kennington road .... 33, C D ; 34, A
    "   *"* Pentonville .... 10, C ; 14, B
    "   street,   do.   .... 10, D ; 14, B
    "   *"* Walworth road .... 33, D ; 34, A
Pentonville cottages .... 14, D
    " hill .... 10, C D ; 14, B ; 16, A
Pepper street .... 27, A
Percival street .... 15, C
Percy circus .... 10, C
    " street, Great .... 10, C
    "   *"* St. Pancras .... 13, B
    "   *"* Tottenham court road........... 6, D ; 7, A
Perkin's row, Westminster .... 4, A
Perry street .... 13, A
Peter street, Clerkenwell .... 10, B
    "   *"* Deptford .... 30, C
    "   *"* Southwark bridge road .... 27, A
    "   *"* Sun street, Bishopsgate................ 18, B

Peter street, Walworth .... Plate 34, B
     "   "   Wardour street, Soho .... 6, C ; 7, A
     "   "   Great, Westminster ....4, A
     "   "   Little,   do.   ....4, A
     "   "   New,   do.   ....4, A
Peter's hill ....1, A
Phelps street...34, B
Phené street ....5, C
Philip street, Back Church lane............ 22, C ; 25, A
     "   "   Shadwell ....25, A
Phillipp's street, Kingsland road ....19, A
Philpot lane ....22, B
     "   street ....23, B; 25, A
Phipps street ....18, C D
Phœbe street ....26, B
Phœnix place, Clerkenwell ....10, C
     "   street, Clarendon square .... 11, B; 13, A
     "   "   Spitalfields ....18, D; 20, B
Piccadilly...................................1, D; 2, B C D
Pickard street ....15, C
Pickering place, Westbourne grove.................. 9, D
     "   street ....16, B
Pickett street ....1, B
Pickle-herring street ....28, A
Pierrepoint row....................10, D; 15, C; 17, A
Pigott street ....26, A
Pilgrim street, Ludgate street ....6, A
     "   "   Upper Kennington lane ....35, C
Pitfield street ....18, C
Pitman's buildings, John's row, St. Luke's ....15, D
Pitt street, Old Kent road ....31, B; 34, A
     "   "   St. George's road ....33, B
     "   "   Tottenham court road................7, B
     "   "   Wyndham road ....33, C
Pitt's head mews ....2, D
Platina street ....15, B
Platt street ....13, B
Playhouse yard, Whitecross street...................15, B
Pleasant place, Bonner street, Bethnal-green ... 24, A
     "   "   Hackney ....21, D
     "   "   Islington ....16, B
     "   "   West square .... 23, B; 35, A
     "   row, Islington ....17, C
     "   "   Lower Kennington lane, 33, D; 35, A
     "   "   Marylebone............................11, C
     "   "   Walworth ....31, B; 33, A; 34, A
Plough road....................................29, B D; 30, A
     "   street ....22, C
Plumber street ....15, D; 18, C
Plummers row ....22, C; 23, B
Pomeroy street ....32, B D
Poland street ....7, A
Pollard row, Bethnal-green road ....20, B
     "   street ....20, B
Polygon ....11, B
Pond place, Fulham road ....5, D
     "   lane, Bankside .... 1, A ; 27, B
     "   "   Clapton ....21, D
Ponsonby place, Millbank ....4, C
     "   terrace, do.   ....4, C
Pont street ....3, A ; 5, B
Pool street ....17, B
     "   terrace, City road ....15, D
Pope's head alley, Cornhill ....18, B
Popham street ....17, A
Poplar market ....26, A
     "   row, New Kent road..................31, B; 33, B
Porchester gardens ....9, D
     "   square ....9, D
     "   street ....8, A; 9, B
     "   terrace, Bayswater ....9, C D
Porter street ....2, B; 6, C
Porteus road ....8, A
Portland market ....8, B
     "   place, Bridge street, Mile-end road ....23, C
     "   "   New Kent road ....31, A B
     "   "   Regent's park .... 7, B; 11, C
     "   road....................................7, B; 11, C
     "   street, Commercial road, East, 23, D; 25, C

Portland street, Walworth .... Plate 34, A B
     "   "   Wandsworth road ....36, A
     "   "   Wardour street, Soho...7, A
     "   "   Great ....7, A B
     "   "   Little ....7, A
Portman mews, North ....7, D
     "   "   South ....7, C
     "   place, Globe road ....20, D
     "   square ....7, D
     "   street ....7, C D
Portpool lane ....10, A
Portsdown road ....8, C
Portsmouth street ....6, C
Portugal street ....6, C
Postern row, Tower hill ....22, D
Pott street ....20, D
Potters fields.......................................28, A
Poultry ....15, B; 18, A; 22, B
Powell street..15, C
Pownall road ....19, B; 21, A
Praed street ....8, A; 9, B
Pratt street, Camden-town ....13, D
     "   "   Lambeth ....35, B
Prebend street, Camden-town ....13, D
     "   "   New North road ....17, A
Prescott place, Battersea............................36, D
     "   street, Great ....22, C; 25, A
     "   "   Little ....22, C D; 25, A
President street ....15, C
Preston street ....24, A
Price's street ....27, B
Primrose hill ....13, C
     "   "   park ....12, B; 13, C
     "   street ....18, D
Prince street, Bermondsey ....28, B
     "   "   Deptford ....29, D; 30, C
     "   of Wales' road ....13, D
Princes court, Tyssen street, Bethnal-green ..... 20, B
     "   gate ....3, D
     "   lane ....34, C
     "   road, Bermondsey ....28, D
     "   "   Lambeth ....35, A C
     "   row, Pimlico ....4, B; 5, B
     "   square, Kennington ....33, D; 35, C
     "   "   St. George's, East........22, C; 25, A
     "   street, Bank.............15, B; 18, A; 22, B
     "   "   Barbican ....15, A
     "   "   Bedford row ....6, D
     "   "   Cadogan street, Chelsea .... 3, C; 5, D
     "   "   Cavendish square ....7, A
     "   "   Commercial road, Lambeth ......27, D
     "   "   Drury lane ....6, C
     "   "   Finsbury ....18, C
     "   "   Fitzroy square ....7, B
     "   "   Green street, Stepney ....23, D
     "   "   Hanover square.........................7, A
     "   "   Kingsland road ....19, A
     "   "   Lambeth ....35, B D
     "   "   Leicester square ....2, B; 6, C
     "   "   London road ....33, B
     "   "   Mile-end New-town ....23, A B
     "   "   Rotherhithe.................28, C D; 30, A
     "   "   St. George's, East ....22, C; 25, A
     "   "   Spitalfields ....18, D
     "   "   Stepney green ....23, C
     "   "   Tower hill ....22, D
     "   "   Virginia row..........................20, B
     "   "   Wapping ....25, B
     "   "   Westminster....................2, A; 4, A
     "   terrace, Hyde park ....3, C D
     "   "   Regent's park ....13, C
Princess street, Lisson grove........................8, B
Printers' place, Bermondsey..........................28, D
Printing-house square ....1, B; 10, A
Priory street ....13, D
Pritchard's place, Hackney fields....................21, A
     "   road ....20, C; 21, A
Privy gardens...................................1, C; 4, A
Prospect place, Back road, Kingsland.............19, C

Prospect place, Cambridge heath, Plate 20, C ; 21, A B
      ″   ″   Globe fields .... 24, A
      ″   ″   Rotherhithe............................ 28, D
      ″   row, Bermondsey .... 28, D; 31, C
      ″   ″   Stepney-green .... 23, C
      ″   ″   Walworth road .... 33, A ; 34, A
Providence place, West Ferry road .... 26, D
      ″   row, Finsbury square.......... 15, B; 18, C
      ″   street, North st. Back Church lane, 22, C
      ″   ″   Walworth .... 34, A C
Provost street... 15, D
Prusom's island .... 25, B
Pudding lane .... 22, B
Puddledock .... 1, A
Pulford place, Thames bank .... 4, C
    ″   street .... 4, C
Pulteney street .... 14, B
      ″   ″   Great .... 7, A
      ″   ″   Little .... 2, B; 6, C; 7, A
      ″   terrace, Barnsbury road .... 14, B
Punderson's gardens .... 20, D
Pye street, New.. 4, A
      ″   Old.. 4, A

Quadrant, Regent street.................................. 2, B
      ″   road....................................... 17, C
Quaker street .... 18, D; 20, B
Quebec street, Great....................................... 8, B
      ″   ″   New.. 7, D
      ″   ″   Old... 7, C
Queen square, Bloomsbury................................ 6, D
      ″   ″   Hoxton .... 19, A
      ″   ″   Westminster .... 2, A; 4, B
      ″   street, Bermondsey, New road........... 31, A
      ″   ″   Brompton road .... 3, A
      ″   ″   Cambridge road .... 23, A
      ″   ″   Camden-town .... 13, D
      ″   ″   Cheapside .... 15, A; 18, A; 22, B
      ″   ″   Chelsea .... 5, C
      ″   ″   Clerkenwell .... 15, C
      ″   ″   Curzon street, Piccadilly .... 2, D
      ″   ″   Edgeware road .... 8, A; 9, B
      ″   ″   Golden square .... 2, B
      ″   ″   Green street, Stepney .... 23, D
      ″   ″   Grosvenor square....................... 7, C
      ″   ″   Hackney road............................ 20, A
      ″   ″   Horselydown .... 23, A
      ″   ″   Islington .... 16, B; 17, C
      ″   ″   Kingsland road .... 19, A
      ″   ″   Mile-end, New town .... 23, A
      ″   ″   Oxford street............................ 7, A
      ″   ″   Pimlico .... 5, A
      ″   ″   Pitfield street, Hoxton .... 18, C
      ″   ″   Poplar .... 26, A
      ″   ″   Ratcliff .... 25, D
      ″   ″   Rotherhithe (Paradise street) ...... 28, D
      ″   ″   Do. (River side) .... 29, A
      ″   ″   Seven dials............................... 6, C
      ″   ″   Soho .... 6, C; 7, A
      ″   ″   Southwark Bridge road .. .. 27, A
      ″   ″   Spitalfields .... 20, B
      ″   ″   Tower hill .... 22, D
      ″   ″   Walworth .... 31, B; 33, A; 34, A
      ″   ″   Webber street, Blackfriars road, 27, C
      ″   ″   Westminster .... 2, A; 4, A
      ″   ″   Great, Lincolns Inn Fields .... 6, C
      ″   ″   Little, do.   .... 6, C
Queen street place, Southwark bridge .... 1, A
    ″ Ann street, Cavendish square .... 7, B
    ″ ″ ″ Whitechapel.................... 23, A
Queen Ann's road .... 21, D; 24, C
Queen's crescent, Prince of Wales' road........... 13, D
    ″ gardens..................................... 9, D
    ″ parade .... 5, D
    ″ road, Bayswater........................... 9, D
    ″ ″ Bermondsey .... 28, B; 31, C
    ″ ″ Chelsea .... 5, C
    ″ ″ Dalston .... 19, B D
    ″ ″ Homerton .... 21, D; 24, C

Queen's road, Kensington gardens... Plate 3, D; 9, C
      ″   ″   New cross .... 32, B D
      ″   ″   Peckham .... 32, B; 34, D
      ″   ″   St. John's wood .... 12, B D
      ″   ″   Regent's park .... 13, C
      ″   row, Kennington .... 33, D; 35, C
      ″   ″   Walworth .... 34, B
      ″   terrace, Camden road .... 14, C
      ″   ″   St. John's wood...................... 12, D
      ″   Head lane................................. 16, B; 17, A
      ″   ″   walk, Kingsland road .... 19, A
Queenhithe .... 1, A; 22, B

Radnor place, Gloucester square .... 8, A ; 9, B
      ″   street, King's road, Chelsea.................. 5, C
      ″   ″   St. Luke's .... 15, D
Rahere street .... 15, C
Ramsey street .... 20, B
Randall street .... 26, A
Randolph road .... 8, C
    ″   street .... 13, D
Ranelagh grove.. 5, A
    ″ place, Ranelagh street .... 5, B
    ″ road .... 4, C D
    ″ street .... 5, B
Ratcliff cross.. 25, D
    ″ square .... 23, D; 25, D
Rathbone place, Oxford street .... 6, C D; 7, A
      ″   ″   Upper, do........................... 7, A
Raven row, Spitalfields .... 22, A
      ″   ″   Whitechapel road.................... 23, A B
      ″   street...................................... 23, B
Ravenscroft street .... 20, A
Rawstone street .... 3, A
Rawstorne street .... 15, C
Ray street .... 10, B
Raymond's buildings, Gray's inn .... 6, B; 10, A
      ″   place, Wapping .... 25, B
Red-cross square .... 15, A
      ″   street, Borough.......................... 27, A B
      ″   ″   Cripplegate .... 15, A B
Red Lion square .... 6, D
      ″   ″   street, Clerkenwell .... 10, B; 15, A
      ″   ″   ″   Holborn .... 6, D; 10, A
      ″   ″   ″   Kingsland road .... 18, C; 20, A
      ″   ″   ″   Wapping .... 25, B
Redman's row, Stepney-green .... 23, C
Redmead lane .... 22, D; 25, B
Rees' row, Clifton road, New cross .... 32, C
Reeve's mews .... 2, D; 7, C
Regency square .... 33, D; 35, A B
Regent circus, Oxford street .... 7, A
      ″   ″   Piccadilly .... 1, D; 2, B
      ″   quadrant .... 2, B
      ″   square, Gray's Inn road............ 10, C; 11, B
      ″   street .... 1, D; 2, B; 7, A
      ″   ″   Chelsea .... 5, D
      ″   ″   City road .... 15, D
      ″   ″   Commercial road, East .... 23, D; 25, D
      ″   ″   Mile-end road .... 23, C; 24, A
      ″   ″   Lambeth walk .... 35, A
      ″   ″   Limehouse .... 26, B
      ″   ″   Vauxhall Bridge road................ 4, C
Regent's canal, 8,B;12,A B;13,C;14,A;15,D;17,A B;20,C
      ″   ″   basin, City road .... 15, C
      ″   ″   Limehouse .... 25, D
      ″   ″   ″   Regent's park...... 11, D; 13, A
      ″   ″   ″   Wenlock road .... 15, D
      ″   park .... 11, C D; 12, A B; 13, C
      ″   ″   road .... 13, C
Remington street .... 15, C
Rephidon street .... 31, A
Retreat place, Hackney .... 21, D
Revels row, Southwark bridge road .... 27, A
Rheidol terrace, St. Peter's street, Islington ...... 17, A
Rhodeswell road.................................. 23, C D; 25, D
Rich street .... 26, B
Richard street, Commercial road, East, 22,C; 23,B; 25,A
      ″   Jubilee street, Mile-end............ 23, B

Richard street, Liverpool road............... Plate 16, A
" " Poplar.................................... 26, A
" " Stepney .... 23, D
Richardson street.............................. 28, B; 31, A
Riches place, Deptford lower road .... 30, A
Richmond grove .... 14, B
" road, Dalston .... 19, D; 21, C
" " East, Hackney .... 21, C D
" " Islington .... 14, B
" " Westbourne grove .... 9, D
" street, Edgeware road.................... 8, B
" " Kennington road .... 35, A
" " St. George's road ..... 33, B; 35, A
" " Thornhill square .... 14, B
" " Walworth .... 34, A
" terrace, Clapham road .... 35, C
" " Whitehall.................. 1, C; 4, A
Riding-house lane.. 7, B
Riley street... 28, B; 31, C
River lane, Islington........................... 16, B; 17, A
" street, do. .... 16, B; 17, C
" " Myddelton square .... 10, D
" terrace, City road............. 10, D; 15, C; 17, A
Robert street, Adelphi .... 27, D
" " Bethnal-green .... 20, B
" " Chelsea .... 5, C D
" " Commercial road, Pimlico ...... 5, A
" " Gray's Inn road........................ 10, C
" " Hampstead road .... 11, B
" " Hoxton................................ 18, C
" " Lambeth .... 27, C
" " Oxford street .... 7, C
" " Sidney St., Commercial rd., East, 23, B
" " West Ferry road .... 26, D
Roberts place, Commercial road, East .... 22, C
Robinson place, Deptford lower road .... 30, A
Rochester row, Westminster .... 4, B D
" square ....14, C
" street, Borough market .... 27, B
" " Rochester row .... 4, A B
Rodney row, New Kent road......................... 31, B
" street .... 10, C; 14, B
Roehampton street.. 4, C
Rolls buildings, Fetter lane .... 6, A
" road .... 31, D; 32, A
Rolt street .... 30, D; 32, C
Roman road, Caledonian road .... 14, D
" " Old ford........................ 24, B
Romney street .... 4, A
Rood lane .... 22, B
Rope walk, Limehouse......................... 25, D; 26, B
Ropemakers' fields, do. .... 26, B
" street................................... 15, B
Rose lane .... 25, D
" street, Bethnal-green .... 18, D; 20, B
" " Covent garden............................ 6, C
" " Soho .... 6, C
" " William street, Shoreditch .... 18, D
Rose and Crown court, Finsbury circus .... 18, B
Rosebank road .... 24, B
Roseberry place, Dalston .... 17, D; 19, C
Rosoman street.. 10, D
" " Upper............................ 10, D
Rotherfield street............................... 16, B; 17, C
Rotherhithe New road............ 30, A B; 31, D; 32, A
" street .... 28, C D; 29, A B; 30, A
Roupell street... 27, D
Royal road... 33, C D
" street...................... 27, C; 35, B
" Avenue terrace, King's road, Chelsea .....5, C
" Oak walk, Hoxton .... 18, C
" Mint street .... 22, D; 25, A
Rugg street .... 26, A
Rupert street, Haymarket .... 2, B; 6, C
" " Whitechapel.................. 22, C; 25, A
Russell place, Fitzroy square.......................... 7, B
" Dover road............................ 31, A
" square ....6, D; 11, A
" street, Bermondsey .... 28, B

Russell street, Upp. Bermondsey.. Plate 28, B; 31, A
" " Great, Bloomsbury............ 6, D; 7, A
" " Little, do................................... 6, D
" " Covent garden.................. 1, D; 6, C
" " Great, do.................................. 6, C
" " Sidney street, Mile-end .... 23, B
" " Rotherhithe .... 29, A
Russell's buildings, Wapping .... 25, B
Russia lane................................... 20, C; 21, B
Rutland gate, Hyde park .... 3, B
" street, Bedford square, East .... 23, B
" " Little, do. .... 23, B
" " Brompton road .... 3, C
" " Hampstead road......... 11, B D; 13, A
" " Pimlico .... 4, D
" " York street, Kingsland road ..... 19, A
Ryder's court, Leicester square .... 6, C
Rydon street... 17, A B

Sackville street .... 2, B
Saddlers' place, London wall .... 15, B; 18, A
Saffron hill... 10, A
St. Alban's place, Haymarket.................. 1, D; 2, B
" " road.. 3, D
" " street.................................... 35, A
" Andrew's hill................................ 1, B; 15, A
" " road .... 31, A B
" " street.................................. 6, C
" Ann's lane .... 6, A; 15, A; 18, A
" " road.................................... 35, C
" " street .... 4, A
" Augustine road .... 14, C
" David street .... 31, A
" Dunstan's hill .... 22, D
" George's circus .... 27, A; 33, B; 35, A
" " place, White street, Borough ..... 31, A
" " road, New Kent road............. 31, A B
" " " Pimlico.................... 4, D; 5, A
" " " Southwark...... 31, B; 33, B; 35, A
" " row, Camberwell.................... 34, B D
" " " Pimlico.................... 4, D; 5, A
" " square .... 4, C
" " street, Camberwell .... 34, D
" " " London docks...... 22, C D; 25, A
" " terrace, Camberwell..................... 34, D
" " " Liverpool road .... 16, A
" " " Pimlico .... 5, A
" Helen's, Great .... 18, B; 22, A
" " place, Bishopsgate .... 18, B; 22, A
" James' park .... 1, C; 2, A; 4, A B
" " place, St. James' square.................. 2, B
" " " Victoria park ....20, C; 24, A C
" " road, Blue Anchor road .... 30, B
" " " Holloway...................... 14, D
" " " Old Kent road, 31, C D; 32,A; 34, C D
" " " Victoria park...................... 21, B
" " square .... 2, B
" " street, Islington .... 17, A
" " " Pentonville .... 14, B
" " " Piccadilly .... 2, B
" " walk, Clerkenwell .... 10, D
" John street, Bethnal-green... 18, D; 20, B; 23, A
" " " Clerkenwell .... 10, B; 15, A C
" " " Islington........................... 17, A
" " " road.................. 10, D; 15, C; 17, A
" John's lane .... 15, A
" " place, Abbey road........................ 12, C
" " road .... 18, C
" " square .... 10, B; 15, A
" " terrace, Regent's park .... 12, B
" " wood park............................. 12, D
" " " road .... 8, B; 12, A C
" " " terrace, Townshend road.......... 12, B
" Jude street.................................... 20, B
" Margaret's place, Westminster .... 4, B
" Marks road .... 33, C D
" " street .... 22, C
" Martin's court, Ludgate hill .... 6, A
" " lane .... 1, D; 2, B; 6, C

St. Martin's street .... Plate 1, D; 2, B
 "   "   le Grand .... 6, A; 10, B; 15, A
 " Mary Axe .... 18, B; 22, A
 "   "   square..................... 33, B; 35, A
 "   "   street, St. Mary square .... 33, B; 35, A
 "   "   "   Whitechapel road.............. 23, B
 "   "   at Hill .... 22, B
 " Mary's road, Canonbury .... 16, D
 "   "   "   Queen's road, New cross......... 32, B
 " Michael's alley, Cornhill.......................... 18, B
 " Oswald's place, Vauxhall...................... 35, C D
 " Patrick's terrace, Great Dover street .... 31, A
 " Paul's Churchyard, 1,B; 6,A; 10,B;15,A;18,A; 22,B
 "   "   lane .... 29, A
 "   "   place, Westmoreland road .... 34, B
 "   "   road, Camden-town............... 13, D; 14, C
 "   "   "   Islington...................... 15, D; 17, C
 "   "   square .... 17, C
 "   "   street, Ball's-pond.......................... 17, C
 "   "   "   New North road..................... 17, A
 " Peter's alley, Cornhill.............................. 18, B
 "   "   road, De Beauvoir town ..... 17, D; 19, A
 "   "   "   Mile-end road...................... 23, C
 "   "   street, Hackney road .... 20, A
 "   "   "   Islington................... 15, D; 17, A
 "   "   terrace, do. .... 17, A
 " Petersburgh place, Bayswater................... 9, C D
 " Stephen's square .... 27, A; 28, B; 31, A
 " Swithen's lane .... 18, A; 22, B
 " Thomas Apostle, Great........................... 18, A
 " Thomas' road,   Bow common .... 23, C D
 "   "   "   Hackney............... 21, B; 24, C
 "   "   square,   do.   .... 21, B; 24, C
 "   "   street, Borough................ 27, B; 28, A
 "   "   "   East, do. .... 28, A
 "   "   "   Islington..................... 17, A
 " Vincent street .... 23, D
 Salamanca street...................................... 35, B
 Sale street, Bethnal-green................... 20, B; 23, A
 "   "   Paddington.......................... 8, A; 9, B
 Salisbury court, Fleet street................... 1, B; 6, A
 "   crescent, Agar-town...................... 13, B
 "   "   Walworth .... 31, B; 34, A
 "   lane .... 28, D
 "   place, Victoria Park cemetery .... 24, A
 "   "   Walworth ...... 31, B; 33, A; 34, A
 "   row,   do.   ......31, B; 33, A; 34, A
 "   square .... 1, B; 6, A
 "   street, Agar-town...................... 13, B
 "   "   Bermondsey .... 28, D
 "   "   Lisson grove....................... 8, B
 "   "   New North road ...... 15, D; 17, B
 "   "   Strand .... 1, D; 27, D
 "   "   Walworth .... 31, B; 34, A
 Salmon's lane..................... 23, D; 25, C D; 26, B
 Salter street.. 26, B
 Samuel street, Limehouse .... 23, D; 25, C D
 "   "   Mile-end New-town .... 23, A
 "   "   St. George's, East .... 22, C; 25, A
 Sandford row, Walworth...................... 31, B; 34, A
 Sandwich street.. 11, B
 Sarah street... 18, C
 "   Ann street................... 31, B; 33, A; 34, A
 Satchwell's rents, Bethnal-green..................... 20, B
 Saunders street.. 35, A
 Savage gardens... 22, D
 Saville place, Battersea fields...................... 36, A
 "   "   Lambeth .... 35, B
 "   row, Burlington gardens .... 2, B; 7, A
 "   street .... 7, B
 Savoy street... 1, D
 Saxon road... 24, B
 Schoolhouse lane..................................... 25, D
 Sclater street .... 18, D; 20, B
 Scotland yard, Great.................................. 1, C
 Scott street .... 23, A
 Seabright street, Bethnal-green road .... 20, B
 "   "   Hackney road.............. 20, C; 21, A
 Sea-coal lane................................ 6, A; 10, B; 15, A

 Sebbon street .... Plate 16, B; 17, C
 Seckforde street.................................... 15, C
 Seething lane .... 22, D
 Selby street .... 23, A
 Serjeants' inn .... 1, B; 6, A
 Serle's place.................................... 1, B; 6, A
 Sermon lane, Doctors' Commons............. 1, A; 15, A
 "   "   Liverpool road .... 10, D; 16, A
 Seven Dials.. 6, C
 Seward street....................................... 15, C
 Seymour crescent.................................. 11, B
 "   place, Bryanstone square .... 7, D; 8, A B
 "   street, Euston square .... 11, B
 "   "   Upper, do. .... 11, B
 "   "   Portman square .... 7, D
 "   "   Upper, do. ....7, D; 8, A; 9, A
 "   "   "   West...................9, A
 Shacklewell green .... 21, C
 "   lane .... 19, C
 "   row...................................... 19, C
 "   street.................................... 20, B
 Shad Thames .... 28, A
 Shaftesbury street, New North road...... 15, D; 17, B
 "   "   Walworth .... 34, A
 "   "   terrace .... 4, B
 Shakspeare's walk, Shadwell...................... 25, B
 Shap street .... 19, A
 Sharp's alley, Cowcross street..................... 15, A
 Shawford street ....5, C
 Sheep lane .... 21, A
 Sheldon street .... 9, D
 Shenton street...................................... 32, B
 Shepherd street, May fair .... 2, D
 "   "   Oxford street .... 7, A
 "   "   White's row, Spitalfields .... 22, C
 Shepherds' walk, City road........................ 15, D
 Shepperton street .... 17, B C
 Sherborne lane..................................... 22, B
 "   place, Blandford square.................... 8, B
 "   street.................................... 17, D
 Sherbutt street..................................... 26, A
 Sherrard street ....2, B
 Ship lane .... 35, A
 Shoe lane .... 1, B; 6, A; 10, A
 Shoemakers' row, Ludgate hill............. 1, B; 15, A
 Shoot, The, Maiden lane, Battle bridge........... 14, C
 Shore road .... 21, B; 24, C
 Shoreditch .... 18, D; 20, B
 Short street, New cut.............................. 27, C
 Short's gardens, Drury lane .... 6, C
 Shouldham street .... 8, A
 Shrubland grove .... 19, D; 21, A
 "   road................................ 19, B; 21, A
 Sidmouth street .... 10, C; 11, B
 Sidney square .... 23, B
 "   street, City road........................... 17, A
 "   "   Clarendon square........... 11, B; 13, A
 "   "   Commercial road, East ... 23, B; 25, C
 "   "   Goswell road .... 15, C
 "   "   Green st. Bethnal-green, 20, D; 24, A
 "   "   York road, King's cross, 13, B; 14, A
 Silk street.. 15, B
 Silver street, Globe road........................... 23, C
 "   "   Golden square .... 7, A
 "   "   Notting hill .... 9, C
 "   "   Rotherhithe .... 29, A
 "   "   Stepney .... 23, D
 "   "   Wood street, City, 10, B; 15, A; 18, A
 Simpson street .... 35, D; 36, A
 Single street... 23, C
 Singleton street .... 15, D; 18, C
 Sise lane .... 18, A
 Skidmore street .... 23, C
 Skinner street, Bishopsgate street.................. 18, D
 "   "   Clerkenwell......................... 10, D
 "   "   Snowhill........... 6, A; 10, B; 15, A
 "   "   Somers-town............... 11, B; 13, A
 Sleaford street .... 36, A
 Sloane square....................................... 5, B

Sloane street .... Plate 3, A ; 5, B
" " Little .... 5, C D
" " terrace, Sloane street .... 5, B
Smart street .... 20, D ; 24, A
Smith square .... 4, A
" street, Jubilee street, Mile-end .... 23, C D
" " King's road, Chelsea .... 5, C
" " Marlborough road, do. .... 3, C ; 5, D
" " Northampton square .... 15, C
" " Somers-town .... 11, B ; 13, A
" " Thomas st. Kennington common, 33, D
" " Great, Westminster .... 4, A
Smith's buildings, Long lane, Bermondsey ...... 31, A
" place, Somers-town .... 11, B
" terrace, Smith street, Chelsea .... 5, C
Smithfield, East .... 22, D ; 25, A
" " Lower .... 22, D
" West .... 6, A ; 10, B ; 15, A
" Bars .... 10, B ; 15, A
Smyrk's road .... 31, D ; 34, C
Snowhill .... 6, A ; 10, B ; 15, A
Snow's fields, Bermondsey street .... 28, A
Soho square .... 6, C ; 7, A
Somers place, Southwick crescent .... 8, A ; 9, B
Somerford street .... 23, A
Somerset street, Portman square .... 7, C
" " Whitechapel .... 22, C
Sophia street .... 26, A
South bank, St. John's wood .... 8, B ; 12, A
" crescent, Bedford square .... 6, D ; 7, B
" end, Kensington .... 3, D
" grove, Mile End road .... 23, C ; 24, B
" place, Upper Grange road, Bermondsey, 31, C
" " Finsbury .... 15, B ; 18, A
" " Kennington common .... 33, D
" street, Bethnal-green road .... 20, B
" " Finsbury market .... 18, D
" " " square .... 15, B ; 18, A
" " Grosvenor square .... 2, D
" " Hercules buildings,Lambeth road,35,A B
" " Kennington common .... 33, D
" " King's road, Chelsea .... 5, D
" " Limehouse .... 26, B
" " Long lane, Bermondsey ... 28, B ; 31, A
" " Manchester square .... 7, D
" " New North road .... 17, A
" " Pentonville .... 14, B
" " Upper Grange road, Bermondsey, 31, C
" " Walworth .... 31, B ; 34, A
" " West square .... 33, B ; 35 A
" " Whitechapel road .... 23, A B
" terrace, Alexander square .... 3, C
" Audley street .... 2, D ; 7, C
" Conduit street .... 20, B
" Island place, Clapham road .... 33, D ; 35, C
" Lambeth .... 35, D
" " New road .... 35, C
" Molton lane .... 7, A C
" " street .... 7, A
" Wharf road, Paddington .... 8, A ; 9, B
Southampton buildings, Holborn .... 6, A
" row, Russell square .... 6, D
" " New road .... 8, A
" street, Bloomsbury square .... 6, D
" " Camberwell road... 33, C ; 34, B
" " Euston square .... 11, B
" " Fitzroy square ... 7, B ; 11, A C
" " Mornington crescent ...... 13, A
" " Nine elms .... 35, D
" " Pentonville .... 10, C ; 14, B
" " Strand .... 1, D
" " Waterloo-town .... 20, B
Southgate grove .... 17, D
" road .... 17, C D
Southwark bridge .... 1, A ; 22, B ; 27, B
" " road .... 27, A B ; 31, A ; 33, B
" square .... 27, B
Southwick crescent .... 8, A ; 9, B
" street .... 8, A ; 9, B

Spa road .... Plate 28, B D ; 31, C
Spanish place, Manchester square .... 7, D
Sparrick's row. Weston street .... 28, A
Sparrow corner, Minories .... 22, D
Spencer street, Church road, Shadwell .... 25, A
" " Goswell road .... 15, C
" " Islington .... 16, B ; 17, C
" " Shoreditch .... 18, D
Spicer street, Battersea .... 36, C
" " Spitalfields .... 18, D ; 23, A
Spital square .... 18, D
" street .... 23, A
Spitalfields market .... 18, D
Spread Eagle street .... 26, B
Spring gardens, St. James' park .... 1, D ; 2, A B
" " Vauxhall .... 35, D
Spring garden place, Stepney .... 23, D
" " West Ferry road .... 26, D
Spring grove, South Lambeth .... 35, D
" place, Wandsworth road .... 35, D ; 36, A
" street, Marylebone .... 7, D
" " New North road .... 16, B ; 17, C
" " Paddington .... 9, B
" " Shadwell .... 25, B
Squirries street .... 20, B
Stacey street .... 6, C ; 7, A
Stafford place, Pimlico .... 2, C ; 4, B ; 5, B
" row, do. .... 2, C ; 4, B ; 5, B
" street, New road .... 8, B
" " Old Bond street .... 2, B
Staining lane .... 10, B ; 15, A ; 18, A
Stainsby road .... 26, A
Stamford road .... 17, D ; 19, C
" street .... 27, D
" " Upper .... 27, D
Stanford road .... 3, C D
" street .... 4, C
Stangate, Westminster .... 27, C ; 35, B
" street .... 27, C ; 35, B
Stanhope place, Hyde park .... 7, C ; 8, A ; 9, A
" " Mornington crescent... 11, D ; 13, A
" street, Clare market .... 1 D ; 6, C
" " Hampstead road .... 11, D ; 13, A
" " Hyde park .... 9, A
" " Regent's park .... 13, C
" " Great .... 2, D
" terrace, Hyde park .... 9, A
Stanley street, Milner street, Chelsea ... 3, A C ; 5, D
" " New North road .... 15, D
" " Paddington .... 8, A ; 9, B
" " Pimlico .... 4, D
Stanmore street, Caledonian road .... 14, B
" " St. Pancras .... 13, B
Staple street .... 27, A ; 28, B ; 31, A
Staples inn .... 6, A ; 10, A
Star corner, Bermondsey .... 31, A
" street, Edgeware road .... 8, A ; 9, B
" " Commercial road, East .... 23, B ; 25, A
" " Wapping .... 25, B
Stephen street, Lisson grove .... 8, B
" " Tottenham court road ...... 6, D ; 7, A
Stepney causeway .... 23, D ; 25, C D
" green .... 23, C
" square .... 23, C
Stevens street .... 28, B
Steward street .... 18, B
Stewart's lane .... 36, C
Stuart's grove, Fulham road .... 5, D
Stoke Newington road .... 19, C
Stonebridge road .... 19, A
Stonecutter street .... 1, B ; 6, A
Stone's-end, Borough .... 27, A
Stonefield street .... 16, A
" terrace, Park road, Islington .... 14, B
Stoney lane .... 28, A
" street .... 27, B
Store street .... 6, D ; 7, B
" " Little .... 6, D
Storer street .... 23, B ; 25, A C

34

Storey's gate, St. James' park .... Plate 2, A ; 4, A
Story street .... 14, B
Stracey street .... 23, D
Strafford street.............................. 26, D
Strand.................... 1, B D ; 6, A C ; 27, D
Stranraer place, Edgeware road........................ 8, D
Stratford place, Camden square .... 14, C
    "   "   Upper Grange road .... 31, D
Stratton street............................... 2, D
Strutton ground................................. 4, A
Studd street............................... 16, A
Sudeley street .... 15, C ; 17, A
Suffolk lane .... 22, B
    "   street, Cambridge road .... 20, D ; 23, A
    "   "   Islington.................... 17, C
    "   "   New road, Whitechapel road ..... 23, B
    "   "   Pall mall...................... 1, D ; 2, B
    "   "   Pentonville .... 14, B ; 16, A
    "   "   St. Pancras.................. 13, B
Sugar-loaf walk, Bethnal-green .... 20, D
Sumner place, Onslow square................ 3, C ; 5, D
    "   street, Southwark bridge road .... 27, B
    "   terrace, Onslow square .... 5, D
Sun street, Bishopsgate........................... .. 18, B
    "   "   Walworth .... 31, B ; 33, A ; 34, A
    "   tavern fields................................ 25, B D
    "   "   gap.................................. 25, D
Surrey buildings, Surrey square .... 31, D
    "   canal.........29, B ; 30, C D ; 32, A B ; 34, B D
    "   grove................................ 31, D ; 34, C
    "   lane .... 36, C
    "   place, Rotherhithe .... 29, A
    "   row, Blackfriars road .... 27, A
    "   square .... 31, D ; 34, C
    "   street, Strand .... 1, D
    "   "   Little.................. 27, A ; 33, B ; 35, A
Sussex gardens, Westbourne terrace .... 9, B
    "   place, Sussex square .... 9, A
    "   "   Kensington.................. 3, C D
    "   "   Regent's park .... 11, C ; 12, A
    "   street, New road, Battersea fields......... 36, A
    "   "   Pimlico..................... 4, D
    "   "   Tottenham court road ...... 7, B ; 11, A
    "   square.................................... 9, A
Sutherland square .... 33, C ; 34, A
    "   street .... 33, C ; 34, A
Sutton place, Hackney churchyard.................. 21, D
    "   street, Belvedere road, Lambeth .... 27, D
    "   "   Commercial road, East..... 23, B ; 25, A
    "   "   Soho square .... 6, C ; 7, A
    "   "   Great, Goswell street .... 15, A C
    "   "   Little, do. .... 15, C
Swallow street .... 2, B
Swan lane, Rotherhithe .... 29, B ; 30, A
    "   place, Old Kent road.................. 31, B ; 34, C
    "   street, Church street, Shoreditch, 18, D ; 20, B
    "   "   Great Dover street.............27, A ; 31, A
    "   "   Minories................................ 22, C
    "   "   Old Kent road .... 31, C D ; 34, C
    "   walk, Chelsea .... 5, C
Swinton street.............................. 10, C
Sydney place, Fulham road .... 5, D
    "   street, do.   .... 5, D

Tabernacle row .... 15, D ; 18, C
    "   square .... 18, C
    "   walk .... 15, D ; 18, C
Tachbrook street .... 4, C D
    "   "   Upper .... 4, D
Talavera place, Hackney fields .... 21, A
Tarling street .... 25, A C
Tavistock place, Tavistock square.................... 11, A
    "   square..................................... 11, A
    "   street, Covent garden .... 1, D ; 6, C
    "   "   Tottenham court road ... 6, D ; 7, A
Taviton street .... 11, A
Teal street, Bethnal-green .... 20, B ; 23, A
Teale street, Hackney road.................. 20, A ; 21, A
Temple inn .... 1, B ; 6, A

Temple street, Dalston .... Plate 19, C D
    "   "   Hackney road .... 20, C
    "   "   St. George's road.................... 33, B
    "   "   Whitefriars.................... 1, B ; 6, A
    "   terrace, Trap street, Bethnal-green .... 23, A
Tench street .... 25, B
Tennison street .... 27, C
Tent street .... 23, A
Tenter street, Little Moorfields .... 15, B
    "   "   Spitalfields .... 22, A C
    "   "   East, Whitechapel .... 22, C
    "   "   West,   do.   .... 22, C
Tenterden street........................... 7, A
Terrace, Kennington common...................... 33, D
    "   road .... 21, B ; 24, C
Thames bank............................... 4, C D
    "   street, Lower .... 22, B D
    "   "   Upper..................... 1, A ; 22, B
    "   "   Rotherhithe.......................... 29, A
    "   tunnel .... 28, C ; 29, B ; 30, A
Thanet street .... 11, B
Thavies inn .... 6, A ; 10, A
Thayer street .... 7, D
Theberton street .... 16, A
Theobald street .... 31, A B
Theobald's road .... 6, D
Thomas' place, North street, Whitechapel ...... 23, A
Thomas street, Back Church lane...... 22, C ; 25, A
    "   "   Bethnal-green road .... 20, B
    "   "   Brick lane............ 20, B ; 23, A
    "   "   Cambridge road .... 23, A
    "   "   Commercial road, East .... 22, C
    "   "   Duke street, Lambeth .... 27, D
    "   "   Grange road........................ 31, C
    "   "   Hackney road ... 18, C ; 19, A ; 20, A
    "   "   Horselydown........................ 28, A
    "   "   Isle of Dogs....................... 26, D
    "   "   Kennington common.............. 33, D
    "   "   New Kent road .... 31, B
    "   "   Old Kent road .... 31, A
    "   "   Oxford street .... 7, C
    "   "   Poplar .... 26, A
    "   "   Walworth .... 31, B ; 33, A ; 34, A
    "   "   Waterloo road .... 27, C
    "   "   Whitechapel road .... 23, A
Thornhill crescent .... 14, D
    "   road .... 14, B D ; 16, A
    "   square................................ 14, B
    "   street, Caledonian road .... 14, B
    "   "   Walworth............................ 34, A
Thornton street .... 28, A B
Thrawl street .... 22, C
Threadneedle street .... 18, B ; 22, A B
Three Colt corner, Hare street, Brick lane ...... 20, B
    "   "   lane .... 20, D ; 23, A
    "   "   street, Limehouse .... 25, D ; 26, B
    "   "   "   Old ford .... 24, B
Three Cranes lane .... 1, A ; 22, B
Throgmorton street.......................... 18, A B
Thurloe place, Brompton .... 3, C
    "   square, do. .... 3, C
Thurlow place, Walworth............... 31, B D ; 34, A C
Tibberton square............................... 17, C
Tichborne street, Piccadilly............................... 2, B
Titchborne street, Edgeware road............ 8, A ; 9, B
Titchfield street, Great .... 7, A B
    "   villas, Regent's park .... 12, B
Tiverton street................................ 31, A
Tokenhouse yard .... 15, B ; 18, A
Tomlin's terrace, Limehouse .... 23, D ; 25, D
Tonbridge street .... 11, B
Tooke street................................ 26, D
Tooley street .... 27, B ; 28, A
Torr's terrace, Deptford lower road .... 30, B
Torriano avenue .... 14, C
Torrington place, Torrington square.................. 6, D
    "   square........................... 6, D
Tothill street .... 4, A
    "   "   New .... 4, A

35

Tottenham court road ... Plate 6, C D; 7, A B; 11, A
    "   place, Tottenham court road, 7, B; 11, A
    "   road .... 17, D; 19, C
    "   street .... 7, B
Totton street... 23, D
Tower dock .... 22, D
    "   hill.. 22, D
    "   street, City.. 22, B D
    "   "   London field .... 21, A
    "   "   Seven Dials .... 6, C
    "   "   Westminster road .... 27, C· 35, A
    "   wharf... 22, D
Townsend street .... 31, B; 34, C
Townshend cottages .... 12, B
    "   road .... 12, B
Trafalgar place,   North st. Whitechapel road, 23, A
    "   "   Walworth ...... 31, B; 33, A; 34, A
    "   road,   Dalston.............................. 19, B
    "   "   Old Kent road....... 31, D; 34, C D
    "   square,   Charing cross.............. 1, D; 2, B
    "   "   Chelsea .... 5, D
    "   "   Stepney............................... 23, C
    "   street............................. 31, B; 33, C; 34, A
Trap street .... 20, D; 23, A
Tredegar square .... 24, B
Trevor square .... 3, A
Triangle, Hackney .... 21, A
    "   Old Kent road .... 32, B
Trig lane... 1, A
Trigon grove.. 35, C
    "   road .... 35, C
Trinity lane, Great.................... 1, A; 18, A; 22, B
    "   road.. 29, A
    "   square, Borough .... 27, A; 31, A
    "   "   Tower hill.......................... 22, D
    "   street, Borough.................... 27, A; 31, A
    "   "   Liverpool road..................... 16, A
    "   "   Rotherhithe........................ 29, A
Trundley's lane ....30, D; 32, C
Tudor road.. 21, B
    "   street .... 1, B; 6, A
Tufton street .... 4, A
Tuilerie street ....19, B; 20, A
Tunnel square .... 28, C; 29, B; 30, A
Turk street .... 20, B
Turk's row, Chelsea................................... 5, C
Turnagain lane... 6, A
Turner square .... 19, A
    "   street .... 23, B; 25, A
    "   "   Little .... 23, B; 25, A
Turnmill street... 10, B
Turpentine lane .... 4, D
Turville street .... 20, B
Twyford street .... 14, B
Tyer's gateway.. 28, B
    "   street .... 35, B D
Tyler's lane... 7, A
Type street, Chiswell street .... 15, B
    "   "   Green st. Bethnal-green, 20, C D; 24, A
Tysoe street .... 10, D
Tyssen street .... 20, B

Ulster terrace, Regent's park .... 11, C
Umberston street .... 22, C; 23, B; 25, A
Union buildings, Union street, Kingsland....... 20, A
    "   crescent, New Kent road .... 31, A
    "   place,   Horsemonger lane................... 31, A
    "   "   East street, Walworth.... 33, A; 34, A
    "   road,   Albany road.............. 31, D; 34, C
    "   "   Liverpool road .... 16, C
    "   row,   Horsemonger lane .... 31, A
    "   "   Kingsland road .... 19, C
    "   "   New Kent road............. 31, B; 33, A
    "   "   Rotherhithe .... 28, D
    "   "   Stepney-green .... 23, C
    "   "   Union street, Kingsland, 18, D; 20, A
    "   square .... 31, A
    "   street,   Bishopsgate .... 18, B
    "   "   Borough road...... 27, A; 33, B; 35, A

Union street,   Great, Borough road........ Plate 33, B
    "   "   Boston street, Hackney road...... 20, A
    "   "   Clarendon square .... 11, B; 13, A
    "   "   Cleveland street, Mile-end....... 23, A
    "   "   Grosvenor row .... 5, A
    "   "   Hoxton .... 15, D; 18, C
    "   "   Kingsland road .... 18, D; 20, A
    "   "   Lambeth walk .... 35, A
    "   "   London road .... 33, B; 35, A
    "   "   Middlesex hospital................... 7, B
    "   "   N. Bridge st. Blackfriars, 1,B;10,A;15,A
    "   "   South street, Park lane............... 2, D
    "   "   Southwark.............................. 27, A
    "   "   Whitechapel road .... 22, C; 23, B
    "   "   New, Little Moorfields .... 15, B; 18, A
    "   terrace, Camden-town...................... 13, D
University street .... 6, D; 7, B; 11, A
Upper marsh, Lambeth.......................... 27, C; 35, B
    "   street, Islington .... 16, B C; 17, A
    "   ground street .... 27, D
Uxbridge road .... 9, A C
    "   street .... 31, A

Vale, The, King's road, Chelsea .... 5, C
Valentine place, Blackfriars road .... 27, A
    "   "   Long lane, Bermondsey .... 31, A
Vassal road .... 33, D
Vaughan place, Triangle, Old Kent road......... 32, A
    "   terrace, Ashley crescent .... 15, D
Vauxhall bridge .... 4, C; 35, D
    "   road .... 4, C D; 5, A B
    "   coachfield .... 35, D
    "   square.. 35, D
    "   street .... 35, C
    "   terrace, Vauxhall walk................. 35, D
    "   walk .... 35, B D
Vere street, Clare market.............................. 6, C
    "   "   Oxford street .... 7, A
Vernon street .... 10, C
Verulam terrace, Edgeware road .... 8, D; 12, C
Victoria crescent, Prince of Wales' road......... 13, D
    "   grove,   Bayswater....................... 9, C D
    "   "   Kensington .... 3, D
    "   "   Victoria park .... 20, C; 21, B
    "   park...................... 20, C; 21, B; 24, C D
    "   road.................. 20, C; 21, A B; 24, C
    "   place,   Hackney road............... 20, C; 21, A
    "   "   Old Kent road......... 31, D; 34, C
    "   "   Walworth........... 31, B; 33, A
    "   "   Westbourne grove................ 9, D
    "   road,   Dalston .... 19, B; 21, A
    "   "   Deptford............... 29, D; 30, C
    "   "   Holloway .... 14, D; 16, C
    "   "   Upper, do. .... 14, D
    "   "   Kensington .... 3, C D
    "   "   Kentish-town .... 13, D
    "   "   Pimlico .... 4, B; 5, A B
    "   square .... 5, B
    "   street,   Barnsbury road.................... 14, B
    "   "   Holborn .... 6, A B; 10, B
    "   "   Shadwell......................... 25, A
    "   "   Westminster .... 4, A B; 5, B
    "   terrace, Caledonian road .... 14, D
Victory place, Walworth............................. 31, B
Vigo street... 2, B
Villiers street .... 1, D; 27, D
Villa street .... 34, D
Vincent square .... 4, C D
    "   street, do. .... 4, C
    "   "   Bethnal-green .... 18, D; 20, B
    "   "   Old street road .... 15, D; 18, C
    "   terrace, Islington .... 15, C; 17, A
Vine street, Bloomsbury............................... 6, C
    "   "   Clerkenwell .... 10, B
    "   "   Millbank................................. 4, A
    "   "   Minories.............................. 22, C
    "   "   Spitalfields .... 18, D; 20, B
    "   "   Tooley street .... 28, A
    "   "   Waterloo road .... 27, C

Vineyard walk, Clerkenwell .... Plate 10, C D
Violet hill .... 8, D; 12, C
Virginia row, Bethnal-green............................ 20, B
   "   street.. 25, A

Wade street, Poplar .... 26, A
Wade's place, do. .... 26, A
Wakefield street.. 11, B
Walbrook .... 22, B
   "   buildings, Hoxton .... 15, D; 18, C
   "   street.......................... 15, D; 17, B
Walburgh street........................... 22, C; 25, A
Walcot place, Hackney................................. 21, A
   "   square.................................. 33, B; 35, A
   "   street .... 33, B
Walnut-tree walk... 35, A
Walpole street .... 5, C
Walter street .... 35, D; 36, A
Walton street.. 3, A
Walworth road............................... 33, A C; 34, A
   "   villas, Westmoreland road .... 34, D
Wandsworth road .... 35, D; 36, A
Wapping High street .... 25 B; 26, A
   "   wall... 25, B
Ward street... 35, B
Wardour street .... 6, C; 7, A
Warner place, Hackney road........................... 20, A
   "   street, Clerkenwell .... 10, C
   "   "   Great Dover street................. 31, A
Warren place,   do.   .... 31, A
   "   street, Camden-town .... 13, D
   "   "   Fitzroy square............. 7, B; 11, A
   "   "   Pentonville......... 10, D; 14, B; 16, A
Warwick court, Holborn .... 6, B; 10, A
   "   crescent, Harrow road .... 8, C
   "   lane .... 6, A; 10, B; 15, A
   "   place, Grove-end road .... 8, D; 12, C
   "   "   Warwick road .... 8, C
   "   road, Paddington........................... 8, C
   "   row, Pimlico .... 4, B
   "   square, City................................ 1, B; 6, A
   "   "   Pimlico .... 4, D
   "   street, do.   .... 4, D
   "   "   Golden square .... 2, B; 7, A
Washington street .... 23, C
Water lane, Blackfriars .... 1, B; 10, A; 15, A
   "   "   Homerton .... 21, D
   "   "   Tower street............................. 22, D
   "   street .... 1, B
Waterloo bridge .... 1, C D; 27, D
   "   place, Pall mall .... 2, B
   "   road, Lambeth...... 27, C D; 33, B; 35, A
   "   "   Victoria park............ 20, C; 21, A
   "   street, Commercial road, East, 25, D; 26, B
   "   "   Haggerstone.................... 19, A B
   "   "   St. Luke's............................. 15, D
   "   "   Walworth .... 34, A B
   "   terrace, Islington .... 16, A
   "   "   King's road, Chelsea .... 5, D
Waterside, Upper Thames street .... 22, C
Watling street............................. 1, A ; 18, A; 22, B
Watney street.. 23, B; 25, A
Weaver street .... 23, A
Weavers' lane .... 28, A
Webb street, Bermondsey new road .... 31, A
   "   "   Bermondsey street..................... 28, A
   "   "   Walworth .... 34, A
Webber row, Waterloo road .... 27, A C
   "   street, Blackfriars road .... 27, A C
   "   "   Waterloo road .... 27, C; 35, A
Weedington street.. 13, D
Welbeck street.. 7, A B
Well alley, High street, Wapping .... 25, B
   "   street, Cripplegate .... 15, A
   "   "   Hackney .... 21, B D; 24, C
   "   "   Mile-end New-town .... 23, A
   "   "   Wellclose square .... 22, C D; 25, A
   "   "   common............................... 24, C D
Wellclose square............................. 22, C D; 25, A

Wellesley street, City road .... Plate 15, D
   "   "   Euston square ....11, B
Wellington place, Blackfriars road............... 27, A
   "   "   Deptford .... 30, C
   "   "   Globe st. Bethnal-green.... 20, D
   "   "   Old Bethnal-green road ..... 20, B
   "   "   St. John's wood................ 12, A
   "   "   Stepney............................ 23, D
   "   "   Walworth........................... 34, C
   "   "   Wandsworth road .... 35, D
   "   road, Bow road .... 24, B
   "   "   St. John's wood .... 12, A
   "   row, Bethnal-green .... 20, A B
   "   square .... 5, C
   "   street, Blackfriars road............... 27, A
   "   "   Camden-town................... 13, D
   "   "   Goswell street.................. 15, C
   "   "   Islington.......................... 16, A
   "   "   Kingsland road...... 18, C; 20, A
   "   "   London bridge .... 27, B
   "   "   Neckinger road .... 28, B
   "   "   Newington causeway .... 31, A
   "   "   North street, Whitechapel, 23, A
   "   "   Pentonville... .... 14, B
   "   "   Stepney .... 23, D
   "   "   Stoke Newington road ...... 19, C
   "   "   Strand................................ 1, D
   "   "   North, do. .... 6, C
   "   "   Victoria park...... 20, D; 24, A
   "   "   Winchester st. Waterloo-tn. 23, A
Wells street, Gray's inn road .... 10, C
   "   "   Oxford street........................... 7, A
   "   "   St. George's, Camberwell............ 34, D
   "   tenements, Deptford lower road .... 30, A
Wenlock basin, Regent's canal........... 15, D; 17, B
   "   road.. 15, D
   "   street... 15, D
Wentworth street .... 18, B; 22, C
Werrington street .... 13, A B
West basin road.. 5, B
   "   ferry road, Isle of Dogs........................ 26, D
   "   India dock road .... 26, A B
   "   lane .... 28, D
   "   Smithfield .... 1, B; 6, A; 10, B
   "   square .... 33, B; 35, A
   "   street, Cambridge heath .... 20, C; 21, A
   "   "   Cambridge road............... 20, D; 23, A
   "   "   Commercial road, Pimlico .... 5, A
   "   "   Finsbury circus............... 15, B; 18, A
   "   "   Green st. Bethnal-green ... 20, D; 24, A
   "   "   Neckinger .... 28, D; 31, C
   "   "   North, do.................... 28, D; 31, C
   "   "   South, do. .... 28, D
   "   "   Seven dials .... 6, C; 7, A
   "   "   Somers-town..................... 11, B
   "   "   Triangle, Hackney............... 21, A
   "   "   Walworth road .... 33, C; 34, A
   "   "   Well street, Hackney ...... 21, B; 24, C
   "   "   West India dock road .... 26, A
   "   "   West Smithfield............... 10, B; 15, A
Westbourne crescent .... 9, D
   "   grove... 9, D
   "   road...14, D
   "   street, Hyde park .... 9, A
   "   "   Pimlico .... 5, A B
   "   terrace, Hyde park........ 8, C; 9, B D
   "   "   North, do. .... 8, C
   "   "   road .... 8, C
Westbrook place, Eaton square...................... 5, B
Westfield terrace, Deptford lower road............ 30, A
Westminster bridge .... 1, C; 27, C; 35, B
   "   road............. 27, C; 33, B; 35, A
Westmoreland place, City road....................... 15, D
   "   road .... 33, C; 34, B
   "   street, Great Marylebone street, 7, B
   "   "   Kingsland road... 19, A; 20, A
   "   terrace, Westmoreland road..... 34, C
Weston place, King's cross .... 13, B
   "   "   Long lane, Bermondsey .... 31, A

37

Weston street, Bermondsey .... Plate 28, A
  "   "   New, Bermondsey .... 28, B ; 31, A
  "   "   Pentonville .... 10, C ; 14, B
  "   "   Somers-town ...... 10, C ; 11, B ; 13, A
Weymouth street, Hackney road .... 19, B
  "   "   Portland road .... 7, B ; 11, C
  "   "   New Kent road.................. 33, A
  "   "   New North road.................. 17, B
  "   terrace, Hackney road ...... 19, B ; 20, A
Wharf road, City road .... 15, D ; 17, A
  "   "   King's cross .... 13, B ; 14, A
  "   "   North, do. .... 14, A
Wharton street.. 10, C
Wheeler street, Spitalfields.................... 18, D ; 20, B
  "   "   Vauxhall bridge road.............. 4, C
Whetstone place, Lincolns Inn Fields.............. 6, C
Whiskin street.. 10, D
Whitcombe street .... 1, D ; 2, B
White street, Bethnal-green road .... 20, B ; 23, A
  "   "   Borough................ 27, A ; 28, B ; 31, A
  "   "   Houndsditch .... 18, B
  "   "   Little Moorfields....................... 15, B
  "   Conduit street .... 10, D ; 14, B ; 16, A
  "   Hart street, Drury lane .... 1, D ; 6, C
  "   "   Kennington .... 33, D ; 35, C
  "   Horse place, Commer. road, East, 23, D ; 25, C
  "   "   lane .... 23, C
  "   street, Commercial rd. East, 23, D ; 25, D
  "   "   Cornwall road..................27, C
  "   "   Piccadilly .... 2, D
  "   Lion street, Chelsea..............................5, C
  "   "   "   Norton Folgate .... 18, D
  "   "   "   Pentonville, 10, D ; 14, B ; 16, A
  "   "   "   Seven Dials....................... 6, C
  "   Post lane, Old Kent road.............. 32, A B
White's ground, Bermondsey .... 28, A B
  "   lane .... 35, D
  "   row, Spitalfields .... 18, B ; 22, A C
  "   "   Whitechapel road .... 23, A
Whitechapel High street .... 22, C ; 23, B
  "   road .... 23, A B
Whitecross street .... 15, B
  "   "   Upper.............................. 15, B
Whitefriars... 1, B
  "   street .... 1, B ; 6, A
Whitehall .... 1, C ; 2, A ; 4, A
  "   place ....1, C
  "   yard .... 1, C ; 4, A
Whitehead's grove .... 5, D
Whitmore road, Hoxton .... 17, D ; 19, A
  "   row,   do.   .. .. 17, B ; 19, A
  "   street, do.   .... 17, B
Whittlebury street .... 11, B
Wick lane .... 24, D
  "   road .... 21, D ; 24, D
Wickham place, Kent street, Borough, 27, A ; 31, A
  "   "   street .... 35, D
Widegate street.................................... 18, B ; 22, A
Wigmore street.. 7, B
Wild street, Great .... 6, C
  "   "   Little.. 6, C
Wild's rents, Long lane, Bermondsey.... 28, B ; 31, A
Wilderness row, Chelsea.................................. 5, A
  "   "   Clerkenwell .... 15, A
  "   "   street .... 31, A
William street, Albany road, Camberwell .... 34, D
  "   "   "   street, Regent's park ... 11, C
  "   "   Blackfriars.............................. 1, B
  "   "   Brandon street, Walworth....... 31, B
  "   "   Brook street, Bermondsey .... 31, A
  "   "   Caledonian road .... 13, B ; 14, A B
  "   "   North, do. .... 14, A
  "   "   Cannon street road........ 22, C ; 25, A
  "   "   Charlotte st. Blackfriars road, 27, A B
  "   "   East street, Lambeth walk ...... 35, A
  "   "   Great Suffolk street.................. 27, A
  "   "   Green st. Bethnal-green, 20, D ; 24, A
  "   "   Hampstead road.................... 11, B
  "   "   Harper street, New Kent road, 31, B

William street, Hart's lane, Bethnal-gn. ...Plate 20, B
  "   "   High street, Lambeth.............. 35, B
  "   "   Hill street, Walworth road...... 33, C
  "   "   Kennington common .... 33, D ; 35, C
  "   "   Lisson grove .... 8, B
  "   "   Lower Marsh, Lambeth .... 27, C
  "   "   Lowndes square .... 3, A
  "   "   New road, Whitechapel road ... 23, B
  "   "   New North road...................... 17, C
  "   "   Newington causeway .... 31, B
  "   "   Park road, Regent's park .... 12, A
  "   "   Pitt street, Old Kent road...... 31, B
  "   "   St. John st. Brick lane, 20, B ; 23, A
  "   "   St. Peter's street, Islington...... 17, A
  "   "   Shoreditch.................. 18, D ; 20, B
  "   "   South Lambeth new road...... 35, C
  "   "   Wandsworth road.................. 36, A
  "   "   Waterloo road....................... 27, C
  "   "   Westminster............................. 4, B
Wilkes street .... 18, D
Willow street, Globe road............................. 23, C
  "   "   Paul street Finsbury.............. 18, C
  "   "   Rochester row .... 4, D
  "   walk, Bermondsey .... 31, C
  "   "   Tabernacle square................. 18, C
  "   Brook grove .... 34, D
Wilmer gardens, Kingsland road..................... 19, A
Wilmington square.. 10, C
Wilmot square.. 20, B
  "   street, Bethnal-green road................... 20, D
  "   "   Russell square .... 6, D ; 11, A
Wilson street, Drury lane................................ 6 C
  "   "   Finsbury .... 15, B ; 18, A
  "   "   White Horse st. Stepney, 23, D ; 25, C
Wilsted street.. 11, B
Wilton crescent .... 2, C ; 3, A
  "   place, Regent's park .... 12, A
  "   "   Wilton crescent .... 2, C ; 3, A
  "   road .... 4, B D ; 5, A B
  "   street, Grosvenor place ...... 2, C ; 3, A ; 5, B
  "   "   Vincent square ....4, C
  "   terrace, Park road, Old Kent road....... 32, B
Wiltshire lane... 25, A
Wimbourne street.................................... 15, D ; 17, B
Wimpole street... 7, B
  "   "   Upper.................................. 7, B
Winchester street, Agar-town .... 13, B
  "   "   Pentonville .... 10, C ; 14, B
  "   "   Upper, do. .... 14, B
  "   "   Southwark....................... 27, B
  "   "   Waterloo-town.......... 20, B ; 23, A
  "   "   Great, City...................... 18, B
  "   terrace, Agar town .... 13, B
Windmill lane, Camberwell .... 33, C ; 34, B
  "   "   Deptford lower road .... 29, D ; 30, C
  "   row, Kennington cross............... 35, C
  "   street, Church street, Lambeth..... 35, B
  "   "   Finsbury square ....15, B ; 18, C
  "   "   Hackney road .... 20, A
  "   "   New cut .... 27, C
  "   "   Tottenham court road .... 6, D ; 7, B
  "   "   Great .... 2, B ; 6, C
Windsor street, City road............................. 15, D
  "   "   Islington .... 16, B ; 17, A
  "   terrace, City road .... 15, D
Winsley street .... 7, A
Woburn place, Russell square .... 6, D ; 11, A
  "   "   Upper.......................... 11, A B
  "   square..................................... 6, D ; 11, A
Wolverley street, Bethnal-green road.............. 20, D
  "   "   Hackney road...................... 20, A
Wood street, Bethnal-green .... 20, B ; 23, A
  "   "   Cheapside .... 10, B ; 15, A ; 18, A
  "   "   Clerkenwell ....10, C D
  "   "   Marlborough road, Chelsea .... 5, D
  "   "   Prince's road, Lambeth .... 35, A
  "   "   Spitalfields .... 18, D
  "   "   Westminster......................... 4, A
Wood's buildings, East st. Walworth ... 31, B ; 34, C

Woodbridge street .... Plate 10, D ; 15, C
Woodland street .... 19, C
Woodstock street .... 7, A
    "   *"* Great.................................... 7, D
Wootton street... 27, C D
Worcester street, Old Gravel lane .... 25, B
    "   *"* Union street, Borough .... 27, B
Wormwood street............................... 18, B ; 22, A
Woronzow road .... 12, B
Worship street... 18, C D
Wright's buildings, Spa road .... 28, D ; 31, C
Wych street... 1, B D ; 6, C
Wycombe street.. 17, B
Wyndham place, Bryanstone square........ 7, D ; 8, B
    "   road .... 33, C ; 34, B
Wynyatt street.. 15, C

Yardley street .... 10, C
Yeoman's row, Brompton road .... 3, C
York gate, Regent's park .... 11, C
  " grove, Queen's road, New cross............. 32, B
  " place, Barnsbury park........................ 14, D
  "   *"*   Battersea fields........................ 36, C
  "   *"*   Portman square .... 7, D
  "   *"*   Lower, do. .... 7, D
  "   *"*   Rhodeswell road....................... 23, C
  "   *"*   St. John's wood......................... 12, B
  "   *"*   Upper, do.................................. 12, B
  " road, Albany road, Camberwell, 31, D ; 34, C
  "   *"*   City road............................. 15, C D
  "   *"*   Commercial road, East..... 23, D ; 25, D
  "   *"*   King's cross.......... 10, C ; 13, B ; 14, A
  "   *"*   Lambeth.............. 1, C ; 27, C D ; 35, B
  " square .... 23, D ; 25, D

York street, Battersea fields................ Plate 36, A
  "   *"* Bedford sq. East .... 23, B ; 25, A C
  "   *"* Blackfriars road....................... 27, B
  "   *"* Borough .... 27, B
  "   *"* Bricklayers' arms .... 31, A
  "   *"* Camden-town .... 13, D
  "   *"* Church street, Shoreditch, 18, D ; 20, B
  "   *"* City road................................. 15, C
  "   *"* Commercial road, East ..... 22, C ; 23, B
  "   *"* East, do. .... 23, D ; 25, D
  "   *"* West, do. .... 23, D ; 25, D
  "   *"* Covent garden............................. 1, D
  "   *"* Globe road .... 20, D
  "   *"* Great, Hackney road .... 19, B ; 20, A
  "   *"* Hans place, Chelsea .... 3, A
  "   *"* John street, Walworth .... 31, B ; 34, A
  "   *"* Kingsland road.......................... 19, A B
  "   *"* London road .... 33, B
  "   *"* Montague square .... 7, D ; 8, B
  "   *"* Upper, do.......................... 7, D ; 8, B
  "   *"* Pentonville..................... 10, C ; 14, B
  "   *"* Rotherhithe .... 29, B ; 30, A
  "   *"* Lower, do................................. 29, A
  "   *"* St. James' square........................ 2, B
  "   *"* Walworth road ..... 31, B ; 33, A ; 34, A
  "   *"* Westminster............................... 4, B
  "   *"* York road, Lambeth .... 27, C ; 35, B
  " terrace, Albany road, Camberwell .... 34, D
  "   *"* Chelsea .... 5, C
  "   *"* Regent's park .... 11, C
  "   *"* Westminster............................... 4, B
Young street... 3, D

Zoar street... 27, B

ADDENDA.

Bath street, North st., Whitechapel road...Plate 23, A
Brewer street, Golden square............................. 2, B
Bridge road, Grove road, Mile-end road........... 24, A
Broad court, Drury lane .... 6, C
Broad sanctuary, Westminster........................... 4, A
Bunhill row .... 15, B
Burying-ground Passage, Paddington street....... 7, D
Caroline street, Hackney road .... 20, A
Cecil street, Strand............................... 1, D ; 27, D
Chancery lane .... 6, A
Charles street, Harper street, New Kent road... 31, B
Church road, Homerton .... 24, D
    "   street, Bethnal-green......................... 20, B
Clare street, Hackney road .... 20, C
Clephane road .... 17, C
Collingwood street, Camberwell .... 33, C
Cross street, Suffolk street, Cambridge road..... 23, A
    "   *"* Great George street, Bermondsey.. 28, B
Dean street, Tooley street .... 28, A
Dolphin lane, Poplar...................................... 26, A
Eleanor road .... 21, A
Farnham place, Gravel lane, Southwark .... 27, B
Fleur-de-lis street .... 18, D
Great Suffolk street .... 31, A ; 33, B
Green street, Bedford row .... 10, A C
Homerton lane... 24, D
Joseph street... 25, C D
King street, Hoxton square .... 18, C

King's place, Pancras road .... Plate 13, B
Lambeth Mews .... 35, B
Little St. James' street, St. James' square ..... 2, A B
London street, Commercial docks .... 29, D
    "   *"* Hackney road .... 20, A
Marsh street .... 26, D
Matilda street, Caledonian road .... 14, B
    "   *"* Old Bethnal-green road .... 20, C
Melina place, Andrews road .... 21, A
New street, Old street, St. Luke's .... 15, D
Orchard place, Orchard street, Portman square.. 7, C
Rivers street, York road, Battle-bridge.. 13, B ; 14, A
St. James' street, Old Kent road .... 32, A B
Serle street .... 6, A
Sion square .... 23, B
Stockwell street .... 32, B
Stratford place, Oxford street....................... 7, C
Russell street, Chelsea .... 5, D
Surrey terrace, Park road, Old Kent road, 32, B ; 34, D
Sylvan grove, Old Kent road .... 32, B
Symons street .... 5, D
Tyssen street, Dalston .... 19, C
Ufton road .... 17, D
    " grove .... 17, D
Underwood street .... 23, A
Union street, St. Paul's square .... 17, A
Wellington street, Chelsea.............................. 5, C

PUBLIC BUILDINGS, &c.

Admiralty, Whitehall .... Plate 1, C ; 2, A
Almshouses, Stepney churchyard... 23, D
Angel Inn, High street, Islington .... 10, D ; 15, C ; 16, A ; 17, A
Apsley House, Piccadilly... 2, C ; 3, A
Artillery Ground, Artillery place, Finsbury square .... 15, B
Asylum for Female Orphans, Westminster road .... 27, C ; 35, A
     "   the Deaf and Dumb, Old Kent road .... 31, B ; 34, C
Auction Mart, Bartholomew lane Threadneedle street .... 22, B
Bakers' Almshouses, St. Thomas square, Hackney .... 21, D ; 24, C
Bancroft's Almshouses, Mile-end road.. 23, C ; 24, A
Bank of England, Threadneedle street.. 15, B ; 18, A ; 22, B
Barclay and Perkins' Brewery, Park street, Bankside... 27, B
Barracks, Upper Albany street, Regent's park... 11, D ; 13, C
     "   Kensington gardens,.. 3, D
     "   Knightsbridge.. 3, B
     "   Ordnance road, St. John's wood .... 12, B D
     "   St. James' park.. 2, A ; 4, B
Baths and Wash-houses, George street, New road.. 11, A
     "   "   Goulston street, Whitechapel... 22, C
     "   "   St. Anne street, Westminster.. 4, A
Beaumont Literary Institution, Beaumont square .... 23, C
Bermondsey Workhouse, Russell street, Bermondsey .... 28, B
Bethlehem Hospital for Lunatics, Lambeth road .... 33, B ; 35, A
Bethnal-green Union-house, Victoria park... 20, C ; 21, B
Billingsgate Market, Lower Thames street.. 22, B
Bloomsbury County Court, Portland road... 7, B ; 11, C
Board of Control, Cannon row, Westminster .... 2, A
Bookbinders' Provident Asylum, Ball's-pond road... 17, D
Botanic Garden, Queen's road, Chelsea... 5, C
Brecknock Arms Inn, Camden road .... 14, C
Bricklayers' Almshouses, King Henry's walk, Ball's-pond road................................... 17, D
Bricklayers' Arms Inn, Old Kent road.. 31, A
British Museum, Great Russell street, Bloomsbury.. 6, D
Brompton County Court, Sloane street, Chelsea.. 5, B
Buckingham Palace, St. James' park .... 2, C ; 4, B ; 5, B
Bunhill Fields Burial-ground, City road .... 15, B
Caledonian Asylum, Caledonian road... 14, D
Calvert's Brewery, Upper Thames street.. 22, B
Canonbury Tower, Canonbury square.. 16, D
Chalk Farm, Regent's park road .... 13, C
Charter House, Charter House square.. 15, A
Chelsea Hospital, Queen's road, Chelsea.. 5, C
     "   Waterworks, Thames bank .... 4, D
     "   Workhouse, Arthur street, Chelsea.. 5, C
Christ's Hospital, Newgate street.. 1, B ; 6, A ; 10, B ; 15, A
*CHURCHES.—*Christ Church*, Battersea fields.. 36, C
     Christ Church, Highbury grove.. 16, D
     St. Botolph, Aldgate High street.. 22, C
     St. Botolph, Bishopsgate street.. 22, A
     St. Bride (otherwise *St. Bridget*), Fleet street....................................... 1, B ; 6, A
     St. Clement Danes, Strand... 1, B
     St. Dunstan, Fleet street.. 6, A
     St. Dunstan, High street, Stepney .... 23, D
     St. George, Wells street, Camberwell... 34, D
     St. George in the East, Cannon street, London dock .... 22, C ; 25, A
     St. George the Martyr, High street, Borough .... 27, A ; 31, A
     St. Giles in the Fields, High street, Oxford street... 7, A
     St. James, corner of Spa road, Bermondsey .... 28, D ; 31, C
     St. James the Less, Bonner's fields, Victoria park.. 24, A
     St. John, Bethnal-green.. 20, D
     St. John, Church street, Hackney... 21, D
     St. John, Church street, Horselydown.. 28, A
     St. John, St. John's wood road, Paddington.. 12, A
     St. John of Jerusalem, Grove street, South Hackney................................. 21, B ; 24, C
     St. Leonard, Shoreditch .... 18, D ; 20, B

---

* All the churches and chapels are marked on the maps thus, +.

CHURCHES.— *St. Luke*, Old street .... Plate 15, D
    St. Luke, Robert street, Chelsea .... 5, D
    St. Margaret, Palace yard, Westminster... 4, A
    St. Mark, Kensington common... 33, D; 35, C
    St. Martin in the Fields, Trafalgar square... 1, D
    St. Mary, Brunswick street, Haggerstone.. 19, B
    St. Mary, Church street, Lambeth.. 35, B
    St. Mary, Church street, Rotherhithe... 28, C; 29, B
    St. Mary, Paddington green... 8, A
    St. Mary, Upper street, Islington .... 16, B; 17, A
    St. Mary, Whitechapel road .... 22, C; 23, B
    St. Mary Abbott, High street, Kensington... 3, D
    St. Mary-le-bonne, New road... 11, C
    St. Mary-le-bow, Cheapside... 10, B; 15, A
    St. Mary Magdalene, Bermondsey street... 28, B; 31, A
    St. Matthew, Church row, Bethnal-green... 20, B; 23, A
    St. Olave, Tooley street.. 27, B; 28, A
    St. Pancras (old church), Pancras road .... 13, B
    ST. PAUL'S CATHEDRAL, St. Paul's churchyard .... 1, B; 6, A, 10, B; 15, A; 18, A; 22, B
    St. Paul, Lower road, Islington... 17, C
    St. Paul, Nelson street, Bermondsey... 28, B
    St. Peter, De Beauvoir square... 17, D; 19, A
    St. Peter, Walworth road .... 33, C; 34, A
    St. Philip, Richmond road, Dalston .... 19, D; 21, C
    St. Saviour, Wellington street, Southwark.. 27, B
    St. Sepulchre, Skinner street, Holborn.. 1, B
    St. Stephen, Avenue road, Regent's park.. 12, B
    St. Thomas, New Charles street, Hackney road... 20, A
    Trinity Church, Bishop's road, Paddington.. 9, D
    Trinity Church, Brompton road.. 3, C
    Trinity Church, Trinity square, Southwark .... 31, A
Church Missionary College, College street, Islington.. 16, C
City of London Lying-in Hospital, City road... 15, D
    "   "   School, Milk street, Cheapside... 15, A; 22, B
    "   "   Sheriff's Court (County Court).. 18, A
    "   "   Union-house, Bow road... 24, B
    "   "   and Tower Hamlets' Cemetery, Mile-end road .... 23, C
Clergy Orphan School, St. John's wood road.. 12, A
Clerkenwell County Court, Duncan terrace, Islington.. 17, A
    "   Workhouse, Coppice row, Clerkenwell... 10, C
Coal Exchange, Lower Thames street.. 22, D
College of Surgeons, Lincoln's Inn Fields... 6, C
Colosseum, Regent's park.. 11, C
Commercial Docks, Rotherhithe .... 29, A B
    "   Sale-rooms, Mincing lane, Fenchurch street... 22, D
Copenhagen House Tavern, Maiden lane, Battle-bridge.. 14, C
Corn Market, Mark lane, Fenchurch street... 22, D
Crosby Hall, Bishopsgate street... 18, B; 22, A
Custom-house, Lower Thames street.. 22, D
Dalston Literary Institution, Albion square, Dalston .... 19, A
Debtors' Prison, Whitecross street.. 15, B
Drapers' Almshouses, Kingsland road.. 19, A
Duckett's Canal, Old ford... 20, C
Duke of York's Column, St. James' park .... 1, D · 2, A
Dyers' Almshouses, King Henry's walk, Ball's-pond road.. 17, D
East India House, Leadenhall street .... 22, B
    "   London Cemetery, Edward street, Stepney... 23, C
Egyptian Hall, Piccadilly... 2, B
Elephant and Castle Inn, corner of Walworth road .... 31, B; 33, B
Elliott's Brewery, Castle lane, Westminster .... 4, B
Emanuel Hospital, Buckingham row, Westminster .... 4, B
Excise Office, Old Broad street, City... 18, B; 22, A
Exeter Hall, Strand.. 1, D
Female Orphan School, St. John's wood road... 12, C
Fever Hospital, Liverpool road, Islington... 16, A
Fishmongers' Hall, London bridge... 22, B
Foundling Hospital, Guildford street, Russell square .... 6, D; 10, C; 11, A
Framework Knitters' Almshouses, Kingsland road... 19, A
Free Hospital, Gray's Inn road,.. 10, C
French Hospital, Bath street, City road... 15, D
Friendly Female Asylum, Gloucester place, Albany road, Camberwell........................... 34, D
Fuller's Almshouses, High street, Hoxton... 18, C
General Post-Office, St. Martin's-le-grand.......................... 6, A; 10, B; 15, A; 18, A; 22, B
Geological Museum, Jermyn street, Haymarket.. 2, B
German Hospital, Dalston lane .... 19, D; 21 C
Giltspur street Compter, Giltspur street... 10, B; 15, A
Goldsmiths' Almshouses, Goldsmiths' row, Hackney road.. 20, A
Goldsmiths' Hall, Foster lane, Cheapside .... 15, A
Government Emigration Office, Park street, Westminster... 4, A

Government Stationery Office, James street, Westminster .... Plate 2, C ; 4, B
Grand Surrey Docks and Canal, Rotherhithe.. 29, A B D
Gray's Inn and Gardens, Holborn, Gray's Inn lane.. 6, B
Greek Church, London wall .... 18, B
Gresham Lecture Hall, Gresham street .... 15, B, 18, A
Grey Coat School, Horseferry road, Westminster.. 4, A
Guildhall, end of King street, Cheapside.. 15, B ; 18, A
Guy's Hospital, St. Thomas' street, Borough.. 27, B ; 28, A
Haberdashers' Almshouses, Haberdashers' walk, Hoxton .... 18, C
Hackney Old Tower, Church street, Hackney... 21, D
 ″   Theological Seminary, Well street, Hackney... 21, B
Hall of Commerce, Threadneedle street... 18, B ; 22, B
Highbury Barn Tavern, Highbury grove... 16, D
Homerton College, High street, Homerton... 21, D
Hopton's Almshouses, Green walk, Holland street, Blackfriars.......................... 1, A ; 27, B
Horse-Guards, Whitehall .... 1, C ; 2, A ; 4, A
Hospital, Devonshire square, Bishopsgate street.. 18, B ; 22, A
 ″   for Consumption, Fulham road, Brompton.. 5, D
 ″   for Diseases of the Lungs, Bonner's fields, Victoria park................ 20, C ; 21, B ; 24, A C
Houses of Parliament, Palace yard, Westminster.. 4, A
Imperial Gasworks, Gloucester street, Haggerstone.. 19, B ; 20, A
Independent do. Haggerstone lane, do. .... 19, B
Infirmary for Diseases of the Eyes, Blomfield street, Finsbury circus .... 18, B
 ″   ″   ″   King's road, St. Pancras.. 13, B
Ironmongers' Almshouses, Kingsland road.. 19, A
Islington Cattle Market, Lower road, Islington.. 17, C
 ″   Literary Institution, Wellington street, Upper street, Islington .... 16, A
 ″   Workhouse, Liverpool road, Islington .... 16, A
Jews' Burial-ground, Grove street, Hackney... 21, B ; 24, C
 ″   ″   North street, Whitechapel.. 23, A
 ″   ″   Mile-end road.. 24, A
 ″   Hospital, Mile-end road .... 23, C
 ″   Orphan Asylum, St. Mark's street, Whitechapel.. 22, C
Kensington Palace, Kensington gardens.. 3, D ; 9, C
King's College, Strand... 1, D
Kingsland Gate, Kingsland road .... 17, D
Lambeth County Court, Camberwell New road... 33, C
 ″   Palace, Bishop's walk, Lambeth .... 35, B
 ″   Workhouse, Princes road, do. .... 35, A
Laycock's Dairy Farm, Liverpool road, Islington... 16, C
Leather Market, New Weston street, Bermondsey... 28, B ; 31, A
Licensed Victuallers' Asylum, Asylum road, Old Kent road .... 32, B
 ″   ″   School, Upper Kennington lane .... 35, C
Limehouse Cut and Basin, Commercial road, East................................... 25, D ; 26, B
Lincoln's Inn Hall, Lincoln's Inn Fields... 6, A
Literary Institution, Bridge road, Pimlico .... 5, A
 ″   ″   Clifford street, Bond street.. 7, A
London Docks, East Smithfield... 22, D ; 25, A B
 ″   Hospital, Whitechapel road,.. 23, B
 ″   Institution, Finsbury circus .... 15, B ; 18, A
 ″   Orphan Asylum, Lower Clapton... 21, D
 ″   University, Gower street, New road... 11, A
Lord's Cricket-ground, St. John's wood road... 8 B ; 12, A
Magdalen Hospital, Blackfriars road... 27, A, 33, B
Mansion-House, City... 15, B ; 18, A ; 22, B
Marble Arch, Cumberland gate, Hyde park .... 7, C ; 9, A
Marlborough House, Pall Mall.. 2, A
Marylebone County Court, Lisson grove, New road .... 8, B
 ″   Literary Institution, Edwards street, Portman square .... 7, D
 ″   Workhouse, New road... 7, D ; 11, C
Merchant Seamen's Orphan Asylum, Bow road... 24, B
Metropolitan Buildings (Model Lodging-houses), Albert street, Mile-end, New-town........ 23, A
 ″   ″   Do.   do.   Pancras road .... 13, B
 ″   Benefit Societies' Asylum, Ball's-pond road .... 17, D
Middlesex Hospital, Charles street, Cavendish square.. 7, B
 ″   House of Correction, Guildford place, Clerkenwell .... 10, C
 ″   House of Detention, St. James' walk, do. .... 10, D
 ″   Sessions House, Clerkenwell green... 10, B
Millbank Penitentiary, Millbank road.. 4, C
Model Globe, Leicester square.. 1, D ; 2, B
 ″   Prison, Caledonian road.. 14, D
Money-Order Office, St. Martin's-le-grand.. 15, A
Monument, Fish street hill .... 22, B
National Gallery, Trafalgar square .... 1, D ; 2, B
Nelson's Monument, do. .... 1, D ; 2, B
New Cattle Market, Caledonian road and Maiden lane, Battle-bridge................... 14, C
New River Head (Waterworks), St. John street road.................................... 10, D ; 15, C
Newgate Prison, Newgate street.................................... 1, B ; 6, A ; 10, B ; 15, A
North-East London Cemetery, Old ford road, Bethnal-green .... 20, C D

Northumberland House, Charing Cross .... Plate 1, D; 2, A
Old Bailey Sessions House, Old Bailey.. 1, B; 6, A; 15, A
Panopticon of Science and Art, Leicester square.. 2, B
Polytechnic Institution, Regent street .... 7, A
Poplar Literary Institution, Hale street, Poplar.. 26, A
Queen's Bench Prison, Borough road .... 27, A; 31, A; 33, B
RAILWAYS.—*Blackwall* Terminus, Fenchurch street .... 22, D
            "   Limehouse station, Three Colt street... 25, D; 26, B
            "   Shadwell   do.   Church road .... 25, A
            "   Stepney   do.   White horse street, Commercial road, East .... 23, D; 25, D
            "   West India Docks, West India Dock road.. 26, A
       Brighton Terminus, Wellington street, London-bridge .... 27, B; 28, A
            "   New Cross station, New Cross road .... 32, D
            "   Goods station and depôt, Willow walk, Bermondsey....................... 31, D
       Crystal Palace Terminus, Wellington street, London-bridge .... 27, B; 28, A
       Eastern Counties Terminus, Shoreditch .... 18, D; 20, B
            "   Mile-end station, Cambridge road .... 20, D; 23, A
            "   Goods station, St. John street, Brick lane .... 20, B; 23, A
       Great Northern Terminus, King's-cross.. 10, C; 11, B; 13, B; 14, A
            "   Goods station and depôt, York road, King's-cross........................ 13, B; 14, A
       Great Western Terminus, Eastbourne terrace, Paddington .... 8, A; 9, B D
            "   Goods station and depôt .... 8, A C; 9, B D
       Greenwich Terminus, Wellington street, London-bridge .... 27, B; 28, A
            "   Spa road station, West street, Neckinger.......................... 28, D; 31, C
       North Kent Terminus, Wellington street, London-bridge...................................... 27, B; 28, A
            "   New Cross station, New Cross road .... 32, D
       North London Terminus (Blackwall Terminus), Fenchurch street .... 22, D
            "   Bow station, Bow road .... 24, B
            "   Caledonian road station, Caledonian road.................................. 14, D
            "   Camden road station, Camden road .... 13, D
            "   Hackney station, Church street, Hackney .... 21, D
            "   Hampstead road station .... 13, D
            "   Highbury and Islington station, Upper street, Islington.............. 16, C
            "   Kingsland station, Kingsland road .... 19, C
            "   Stepney, White-horse street, Commercial road, East .... 23, D; 25 D
       North-Western Terminus, Euston square .... 11, B
            "   Camden station, Hampstead road... 13, D
            "   Goods station, Haydon square, Minories .... 22, C
            "   Goods station and depôt, Oval road, Regent's park .... 13, C
       South-Eastern Terminus, Wellington street, London-bridge .... 27, B; 28, A
            "   Goods station and depôt, Bricklayers' Arms Terminus, Old Kent road...... 31, D
       South-Western Terminus, Waterloo road... 27, C
            "   Vauxhall station, New Bridge street, Vauxhall.............................. 35, D
            "   Goods station and depôt, Nine Elms .... 35, D; 36, A
       Tilbury and Gravesend, Blackwall and Eastern Counties Terminii .... 18, D; 20, B; 22, D
       Woolwich Terminus (Eastern Counties), Shoreditch .... 18, D; 20, B
            "   Mile-end station (Eastern Counties), Cambridge road.......................... 20, D; 23, A
Raine's Asylum, Old Gravel lane, Wapping.. 25, B
River Thames and Steam-boat Piers 1, 4, 5, 22, 25, 26, 27, 28, 29, 35, 36
Roman Catholic Cathedral, St. George's road, Southwark.. 27, C
      "   "   Church, Blomfield street, Finsbury circus .... 18, B
Rosemary Branch Tavern, Shepperton street, Islington .... 17, B
Rotherhithe Workhouse, Deptford Lower road.. 30, A
Rowland Hill's Almshouses, Hill street, Blackfriars road... 27, A
Royal Botanic Gardens, Regent's park .... 11, C; 12, A
  "   Dockyard, Prince street, Deptford .... 29, D; 30, C
  "   Exchange, Cornhill .... 18, B; 22, B
  "   Humane Society's Receiving-house, Hyde park.. 3, B
  "   Institution, Albemarle street, Piccadilly .... 2, B
  "   Mews, Stafford row, Pimlico .... 2, C; 5, B
  "   Military Asylum, King's road, Chelsea .... 5, C D
  "   Mint, Towerhill... 22, D
  "   Naval School, Lewisham road, New cross .... 32, D
  "   Westminster Mews, Princes street, Westminster .... 4, A
Russell Institution, Great Coram street, Brunswick square .... 11, A
Sailors' Home, East India Dock road, Poplar... 26, A
    "   "   Well street, Wellclose square ....22. D; 25, A
St. Bartholomew's Hospital, West Smithfield.................................. 1, B; 6, A; 10, B; 15, A
St. George's Hospital, Hyde-park Corner.. 2, C; 3, A
    "   Workhouse, Mount street, Berkeley square.. 2, D
St. Helena gardens, Deptford Lower road.. 30, B
St. James' Palace, St. James' park and Pall Mall... 2, B
St. Katherine's Docks, East Smithfield .... 22, D
    "   Hospital, Regent's park .... 11, D; 13, C
St. Luke's Lunatic Asylum, Old street.. 15, D
    "   Workhouse, City road.. 15, D
St. Mary's Hospital, Cambridge place, Paddington .... 8, A; 9, B
St. Pancras Workhouse, King's road, St. Pancras .... 13, B
St. Saviour's Union-house, Marlborough street, Blackfriars road .... 27, C

43

St. Thomas' Hospital, St. Thomas street, Borough .... Plate 27, B ; 28, A
School for the Indigent Blind, St. George's circus, Blackfriars road .... 27, A; 33, B; 35, A
Serpentine River, Hyde park and Kensington gardens.. 3, B; 9, C
Shadwell Basin, London dock.. 25, B
Shoreditch Almshouses, Brunswick street, Hackney road.. 19, B
    "   "   Old street road.. 18, D
    "   County Court, Old street road.. 18, D
    "   Workhouse, Kingsland road.. 18, C
Somerset House, Strand.. 19, A
Southgate Road Chapel, Southgate road.. 1, D
Southwark County Court, Swan street, Great Dover street.. 17, D
    "   Waterworks, Battersea fields .... 31, A
State Paper Office, St. James' park.. 36, B
Stationers' Hall, Stationers' court, Ludgate street.. 1, C ; 4, A
Stock Exchange, Bartholomew lane, Bank.. 10, B ; 15, A
Surrey County Goal, Horsemonger lane.. 22, B
    "   Sessions House, Newington causeway.. 31, A
    "   Zoological Gardens, New street, Kennington road.............................. 31, A
Tattersall's, Grosvenor place, Hyde park corner.. 33, C D; 34, A
Temple Bar, Fleet street .... 2, C; 3, A
    "   Inn and Gardens, Temple street, Whitefriars.. 1, B; 6, A
Thames Tunnel, Rotherhithe street to Wapping High street.......................... 25, B; 28, C; 29, B; 30, A
THEATRES.—*Adelphi*, Strand .... 1, D
           Astley's, Bridge street, Westminster .... 1, D
           Britannia, High street, Hoxton .... 27, C; 35, B
           City of London, Norton Folgate .... 18, C ; 20, A
           Covent Garden, Bow street, Covent garden .... 18, D
           Drury-lane, Russell street,   do. .... 6, C
           Grecian Saloon, City road.. 1, D; 6, C
           Haymarket, Haymarket.. 15, D
           Her Majesty's (Italian Opera), Haymarket .... 1, D; 2, B
           Lyceum, Strand.. 1, D; 2, B
           Olympic, Wych street, Strand .... 1, D
           Pavilion, Whitechapel road.. 1, D; 6, C
           Princess', Oxford street .... 23, B
           Queen's, John street, Tottenham court road .... 7, A
           Royal Standard, Shoreditch.. 7, B
           Sadler's Wells, St. John street road.. 18, D
           Soho, Dean street, Soho,.. 10, D ; 15, C
           St. James', King street, St. James'.. 6, C ; 7, A
           Strand, Strand .... 2, B
           Surrey, Blackfriars road .... 1, D
           Victoria, Waterloo road .... 27, A; 33, B; 35, A
Tower of London, Tower-hill.. 27, C
Treasury, Whitehall.. 22, D
Trinity Almshouses, Whitechapel road.. 1, C; 2, A; 4, A
    "   House, Trinity square, Tower-hill.. 23, A
United Service Museum, Whitehall yard.. 22, D
University Hall (London University), Gordon square .... 1, C
Vauxhall Gardens, near Vauxhall-bridge .... 11, A
Veterinary College, Great College street, Camden-town.. 35, D
Victoria Park Cemetery, Green street, Bethnal-green.. 13, B
Victualling Office and Yard, Grove street, Deptford.. 24, A
Vintners' Almshouses, Whitechapel road.. 29, D; 30, C
Walworth Lecture Hall, Lorimore terrace, Carter street, Walworth road .... 23, A
    "   Literary Institution, Manor place, Walworth road................................ 33, C; 34, A
    "   Workhouse, Westmoreland road, Walworth...................................... 33, C; 34, A
Weavers' Almshouses, Old street road.. 34, D
Wellington Statue, Royal Exchange, Cornhill.. 18, C
Wesleyan Chapel, East India Dock road, Poplar .... 18, A
    "   Hall, Bishopsgate street.. 26, A
West India Docks, Limehouse.. 22, A
Western Literary Institution, Leicester square.. 26, A
Westminster Abbey.. 2, B
    "   Bridewell, Francis street, Westminster.. 1, C ; 4, A
    "   County Court, St. Martin's lane.. 4, B; 5, A
    "   Guildhall, Broad Sanctuary, Westminster.. 2, B
    "   Hall, Palace yard.. 4, A
    "   Hospital, Broad Sanctuary, Westminster.. 4, A
    "   Literary Institution, Great Smith street, Westminster .... 4, A
    "   School, Deans yard, Westminster.. 4, A
Whitbread's Brewery, Chiswell street, Finsbury.. 4, A
White Hall (Banqueting House), Whitehall .... 15, B
White House Lunatic Asylum, Bethnal-green.. 1, C ; 4, A
Whitechapel County Court, Osborn street, Whitechapel .... 20, D
    "   Union-house, Charles street, Mile-end New-town .... 22, C; 23, B
    "   "   Whitechapel road .... 23, A
Widows' Almshouses, Retreat place, Hackney.. 23, B
Zoological Gardens, Regent's park .... 11, D ; 12, B ; 13, C

EXHIBITIONS, &c., IN THE METROPOLIS,

WITH TIMES AND MODES OF ADMISSION.

† Amateur Exhibition of Paintings, 121 Pall Mall.. Open Daily.
* Asiatic Society's Museum, 5 New Burlington street.. Mon. Wed. Fri.
* Botanic Gardens, Queen's road, Chelsea.. Daily.
† Botanic Gardens, Regent's park.. Daily.
British Museum, Great Russell street, Bloomsbury.. Mon. Wed. Fri.
† British Institution (Paintings), 52 Pall Mall.. Daily.
† Burford's Panorama, Leicester square.. Daily.
† Chelsea Hospital, Queen's road, Chelsea .... Daily.
† Chelsea Military Academy, King's road, Chelsea .... Friday.
* College of Surgeons' Museum, Lincoln's Inn fields.............................. Mon. Tues. Wed. Thurs.
† Colosseum, Regent's park.. Daily.
† Cosmorama, 209 Regent street.. Daily.
† Cyclorama, Bazaar, Baker street, Portman square.. Daily.
Custom House, Lower Thames street .... Daily.
Deptford Dockyard, Prince street, Deptford.. Daily.
† Duke of York's Column, St. James's park.. Daily.
East India Company's Museum, East India House, Leadenhall street .... Friday.
† Egyptian Hall (Mount Blanc, and other exhibitions), Piccadilly............................ Daily.
* Entomological Museum, Bond street.. Tuesday.
† Gallery of German Artists, 168 New Bond street .... Daily.
† Gallery of Illustrations, 14 Regent street.. Daily.
Geological Museum, Jermyn street.. Mon. Tues. Wed.
Gresham Lectures, Gresham Hall, Gresham street.. Daily during Term Time.
Guildhall, King street, Cheapside.. Daily.
* Houses of Parliament, Palace yard, Westminster .... Daily.
* Linnean Society's Collection, Soho square.. Wed. and Fri.
* Mansion House, End of Cornhill.. Daily.
Missionary Society's Museum, Blomfield street, Finsbury circus.............................. Daily.
† Model of the Globe, Leicester square.. Daily.
† Monument, Fish street hill.. Daily.
National Gallery, Trafalgar square.. Mon. Tues. Wed. Thurs.
Pantheon, Oxford street .... Daily.
† Panopticon of Science and Art, Leicester square.. Daily.
† Polytechnic Institution, 309 Regent street.. Daily.
† Portland Gallery, 316 Regent street.. Daily.
† Royal Academy (same building as National Gallery), Trafalgar square..... Daily, in May, June, and July.
† Royal Cyclorama (annexed to the Colosseum), Albany street, Regent's park .... Daily.
* Royal Institution Museum, Albemarle street, Piccadilly.. Daily.
Royal Mint, Tower hill.. Daily.
† St. Paul's Cathedral, St. Paul's churchyard.. Thursday.
* Sir John Soanes Museum, Lincoln's Inn Fields .... Thurs. and Fri. in April, May, and June.
Society of Arts, John street, Adelphi .... Daily, except Wednesday.
† Society of British Artists, Suffolk street, Pall Mall.. Daily.
† Society of Painters in Water Colours, 5 Pall Mall.. Daily.
Surrey Zoological Gardens, New street and Penton place, Kennington road .... Daily.
† Thames Tunnel, from Rotherhithe to Wapping .... Always.
† Tower of London, Tower hill.. Daily.
* Tussaud's Wax Work, Bazaar, Baker street, Portman square .... Daily.
* United Service Museum, Whitehall yard.. Daily.
Vernon Gallery, Marlborough House, Pall Mall .... Mon. Tues. Wed. Thurs.
† Westminster Abbey, Palace yard, Westminster .... Daily.
† Zoological Gardens and Museum, Regent's park .... Daily,

IN THE SUBURBS.

† Crystal Palace, Sydenham (Railway from London bridge).. Daily.
* Dulwich Picture Gallery (Omnibus from Gracechurch street) .... Daily, except Friday.
† Greenwich Hospital (Railway from London bridge).. Daily.
Hampton Court Palace and Gardens (South-Western Railway) .... Daily, except Friday.
' Horticultural Gardens, Chiswick (South-Western Railway) .... Daily.
Kew Gardens (North London and South-Western Railways).. Daily.
Windsor Castle (Great Western and South-Western railways)...................................... Daily.
Woolwich Arsenal and Dockyard (Eastern Counties and North Kent Railways)............................ Daily.

---

* Require Tickets.   † Must be Paid for.   The rest are Free.

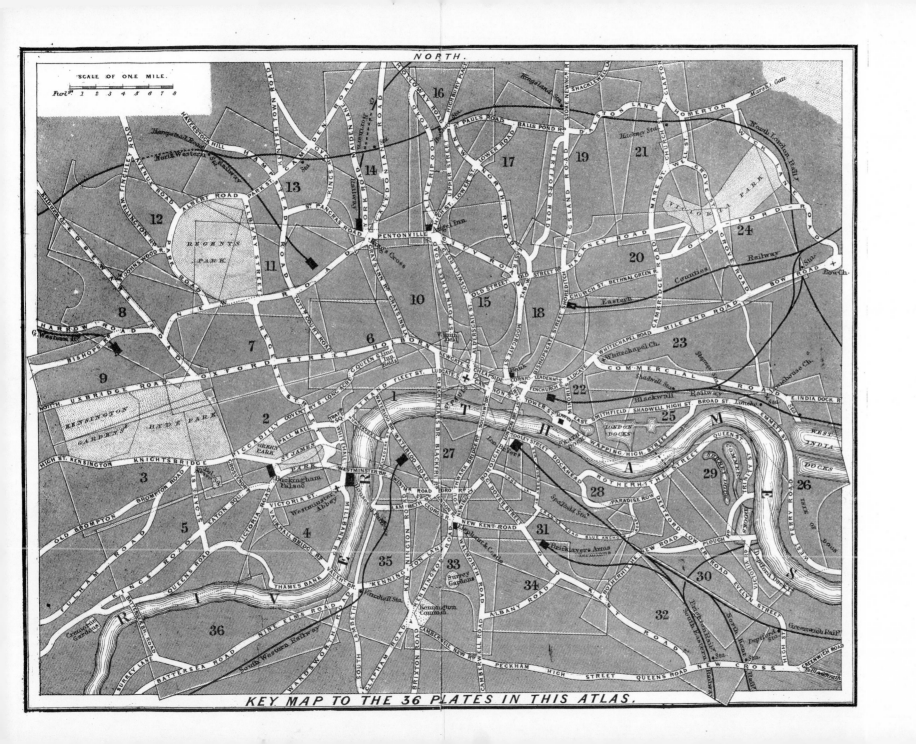

NORTH.

SCALE OF ONE MILE.

KEY MAP TO THE 36 PLATES IN THIS ATLAS.

PRIZE MAPS,

ATLASES, AND GLOBES.

THE ONLY MEDAL AWARDED TO

ENGLAND

IN THE

NEW YORK EXHIBITION,

FOR

𝔐𝔞𝔭𝔰, 𝔄𝔱𝔩𝔞𝔰𝔢𝔰, 𝔞𝔫𝔡 𝔊𝔩𝔬𝔟𝔢𝔰,

WAS TO

MR. H. G. COLLINS,

22 PATERNOSTER ROW, LONDON.

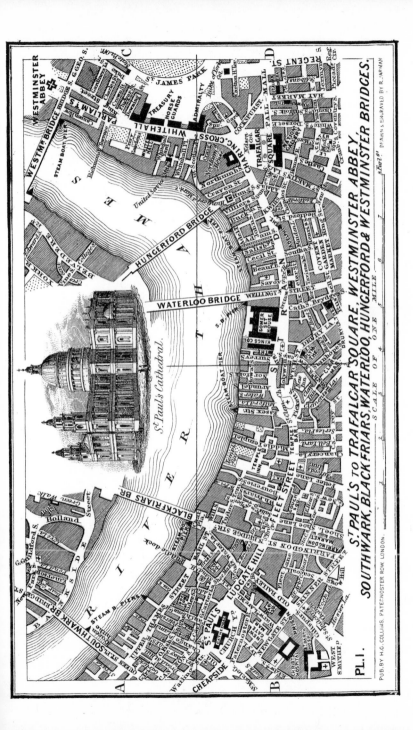

PL. I.

ST. PAUL'S TO TRAFALGAR SQUARE, WESTMINSTER ABBEY,
SOUTHWARK, BLACKFRIARS, WATERLOO, HUNGERFORD & WESTMINSTER BRIDGES.

SCALE OF ONE MILE

PUB. BY H.G. COLLINS, PATERNOSTER ROW, LONDON.

DRAWN & ENGRAVED BY R. JARMAN.

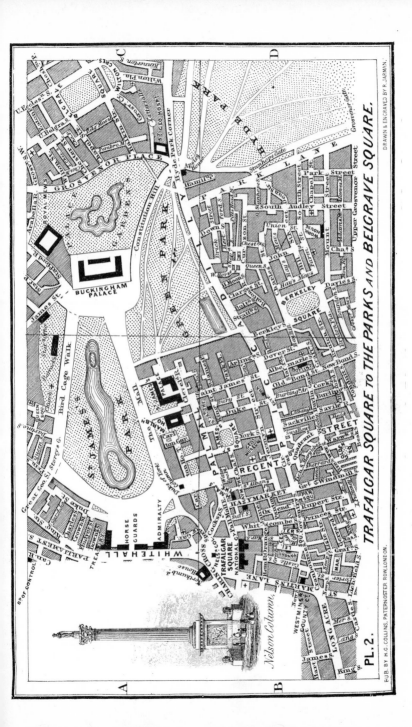

PL. 2.

TRAFALGAR SQUARE *TO THE* PARKS *AND* BELGRAVE SQUARE.

DRAWN & ENGRAVED BY R. JARMAN.

PUB. BY H. G. COLLINS, PATERNOSTER ROW, LONDON.

Nelson Column.

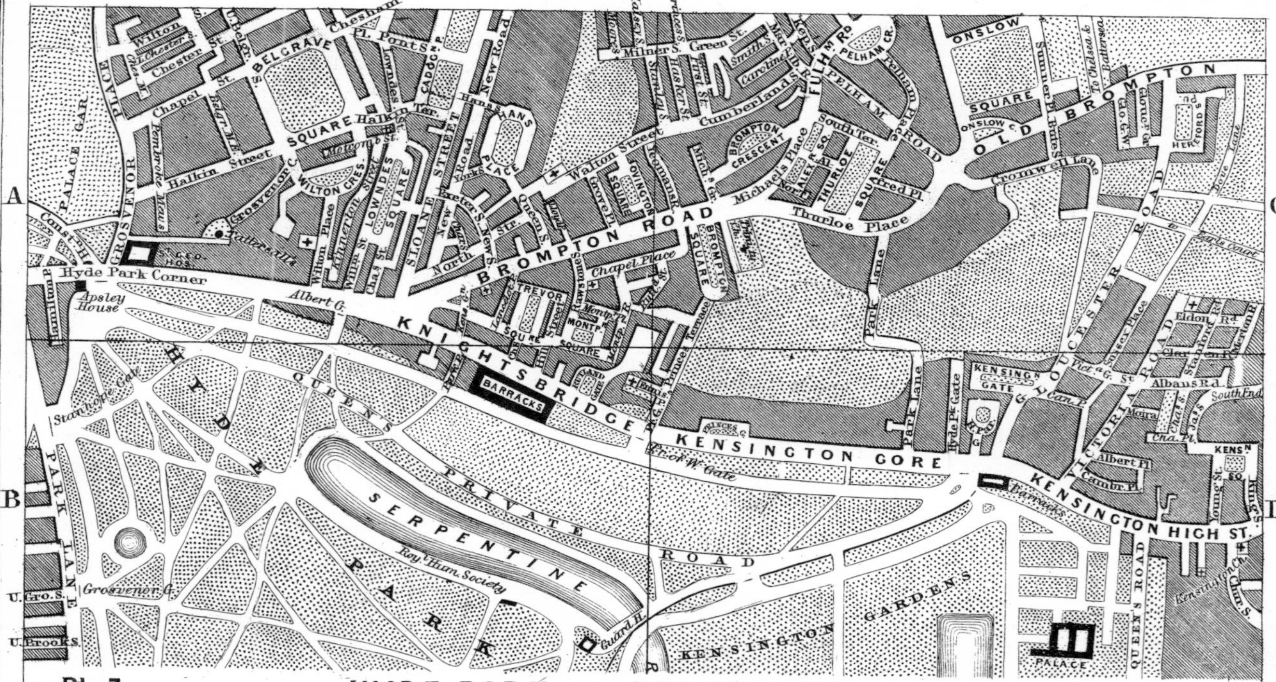

PL. 3.   HYDE PARK TO KENSINGTON AND BROMPTON.

DRAWN & ENGRAVED BY R. JARMAN.

PUB. BY H. G. COLLINS, PATERNOSTER ROW, LONDON.

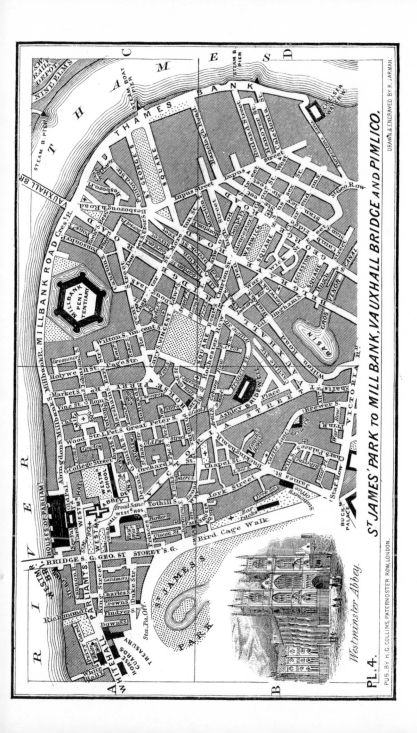

PL. 4.

ST JAMES' PARK TO MILL BANK, VAUXHALL BRIDGE AND PIMLICO.

DRAWN & ENGRAVED BY R. JARMAN.

PUB. BY H. G. COLLINS, PATERNOSTER ROW, LONDON.

Westminster Abbey.

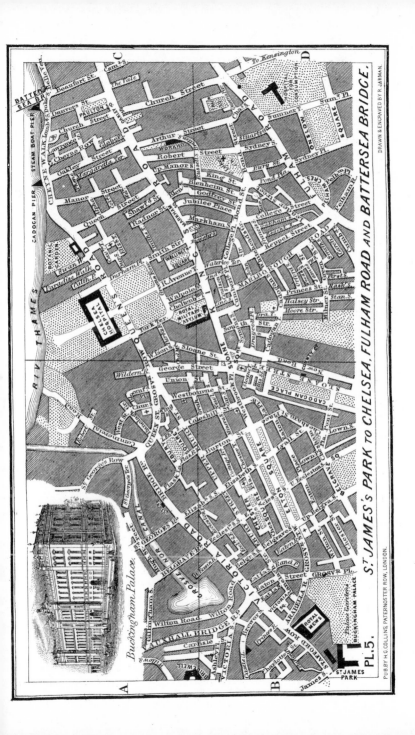

PL.5.

St JAMES's PARK to CHELSEA, FULHAM ROAD and BATTERSEA BRIDGE.

DRAWN & ENGRAVED BY R. JARMAN.

PUB. BY H.G.COLLINS, PATERNOSTER ROW, LONDON.

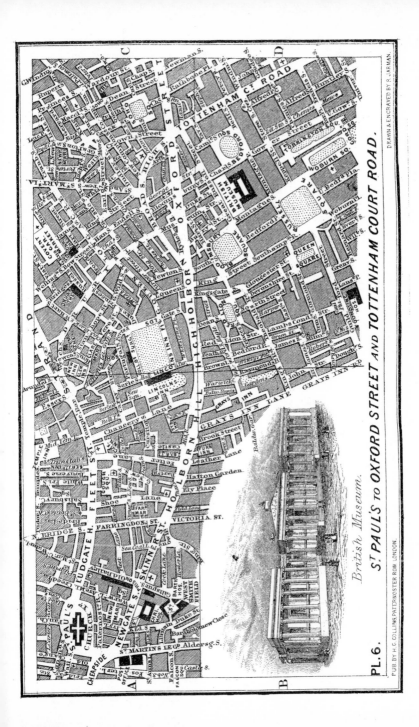

British Museum.

PL. 6.

ST PAUL'S TO OXFORD STREET AND TOTTENHAM COURT ROAD.

DRAWN & ENGRAVED BY R. JARMAN.

PUB. BY H. C. COLLINS PATERNOSTER ROW LONDON.

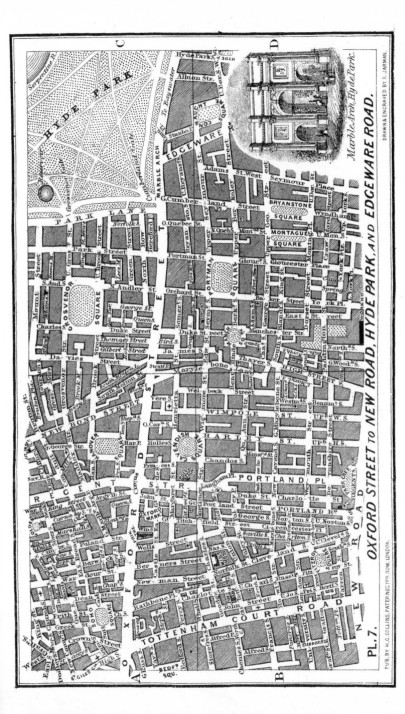

Marble Arch, Hyde Park.

DRAWN & ENGRAVED BY R. JARMAN.

PL. 7.

OXFORD STREET TO NEW ROAD, HYDE PARK, AND EDGEWARE ROAD.

PUB. BY H.C. COLLINS, PATER.NOˢ.TᴿR. ROW, LONDON.

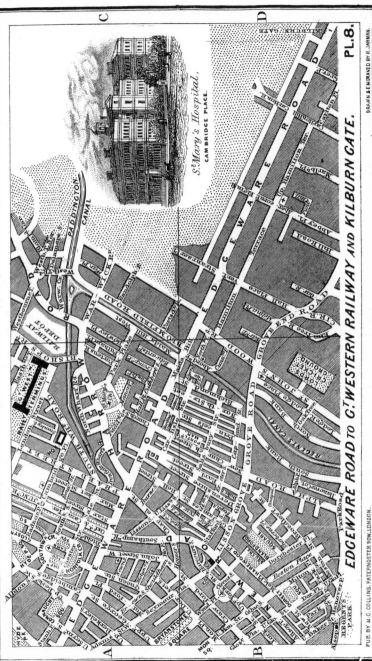

St.Mary's Hospital,
CAMBRIDGE PLACE.

EDGEWARE ROAD TO GT WESTERN RAILWAY AND KILBURN GATE.

PL.8.

PUB. BY H.C. COLLINS, PATERNOSTER ROW, LONDON.

DRAWN & ENGRAVED BY R. JARMAN.

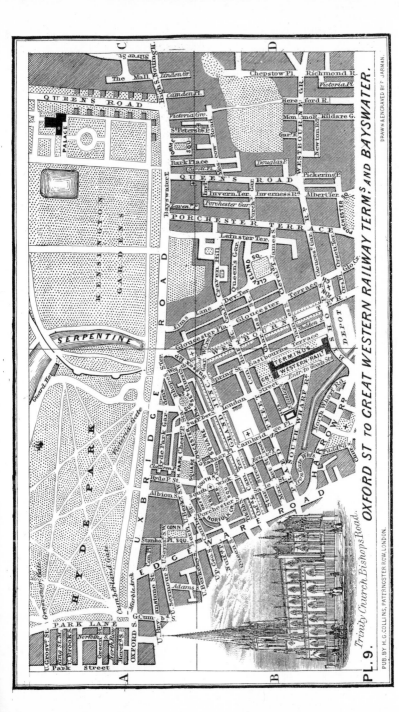

PL. 9.   OXFORD ST TO GREAT WESTERN RAILWAY TERMS AND BAYSWATER.

Trinity Church Bishops Road.

DRAWN & ENGRAVED BY P. JARMAN.

PUB. BY H.G. COLLINS, PATERNOSTER ROW, LONDON.

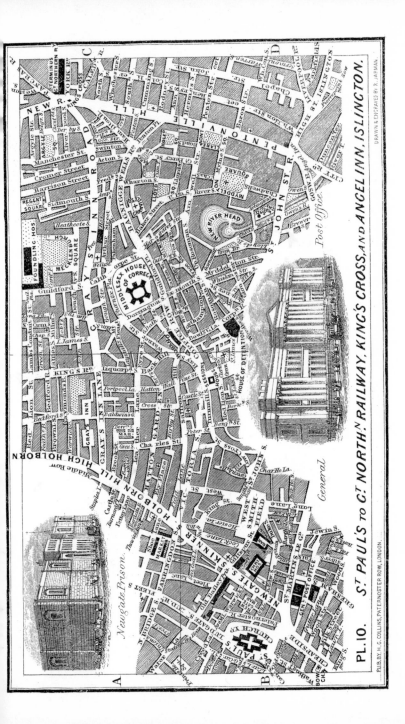

PL. 10. ST PAUL'S TO GT NORTHN RAILWAY, KING'S CROSS, AND ANGEL INN, ISLINGTON.

DRAWN & ENGRAVED BY R. JARMAN.

PUB. BY H. G. COLLINS, PATERNOSTER ROW, LONDON.

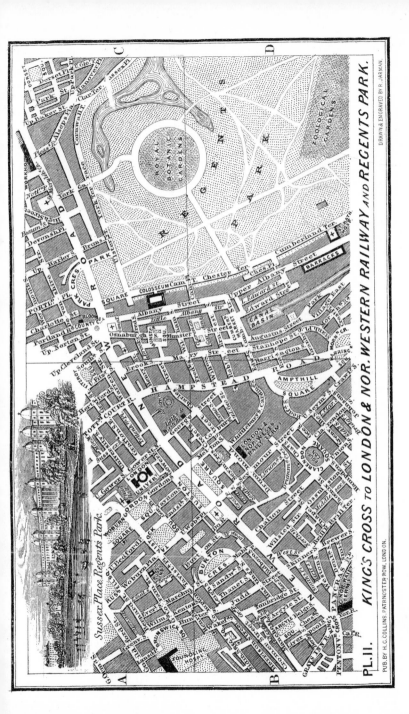

PL.II.   KING'S CROSS TO LONDON & NOR. WESTERN RAILWAY AND REGENTS PARK.

PUB. BY H. G. COLLINS, PATERNOSTER ROW, LONDON.

DRAWN & ENGRAVED BY R. JARMAN.

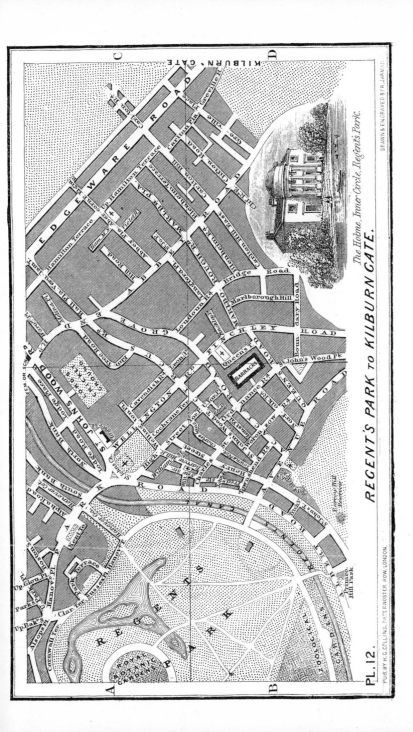

PL.12.

REGENT'S PARK TO KILBURN GATE.

The Holme, Inner Circle, Regent's Park.

DRAWN & ENGRAVED BY R. JARMAN.

KILBURN GATE.

PUB. BY H.G. COLLINS, PATERNOSTER ROW LONDON.

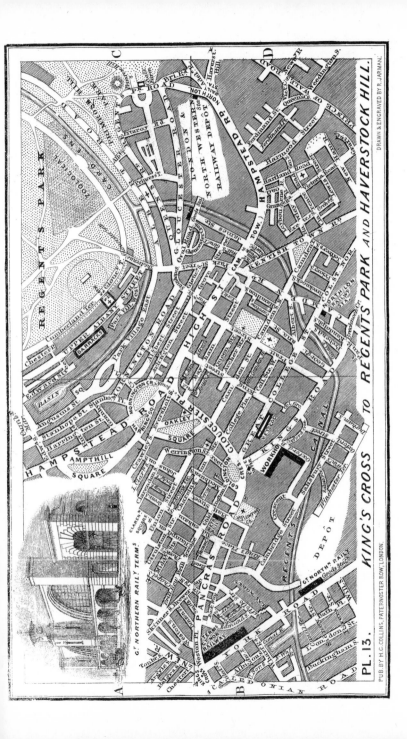

PL. 13.　KING'S CROSS　TO　REGENTS PARK AND HAVERSTOCK HILL.

PUB. BY H.C. COLLINS, PATERNOSTER ROW, LONDON.

DRAWN & ENGRAVED BY R. JARMAN.

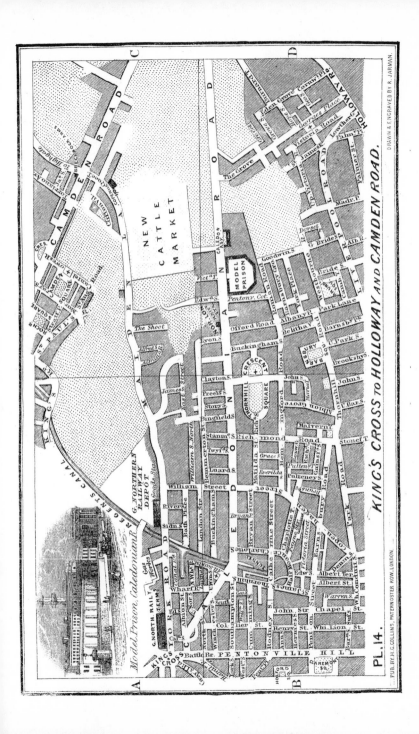

PL. 14.

KING'S CROSS TO HOLLOWAY AND CAMDEN ROAD.

DRAWN & ENGRAVED BY R. JARMAN.

PUB. BY H. G. COLLINS, PATERNOSTER ROW, LONDON.

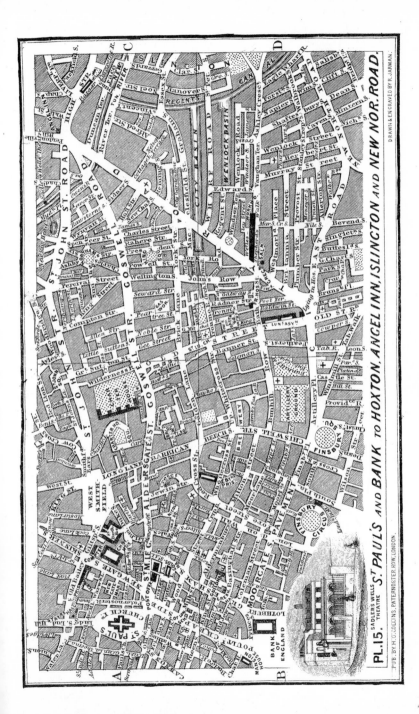

PL. 15. SADLERS WELLS THEATRE ST. PAUL'S AND BANK TO HOXTON, ANGEL INN, ISLINGTON AND NEW NOR. ROAD.

DRAWN & ENGRAVED BY R. JARMAN.

PUB. BY H. G. COLLINS, PATERNOSTER ROW, LONDON.

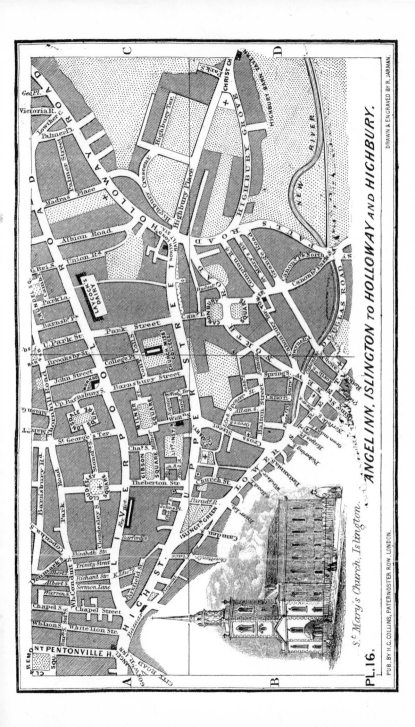

PL.16.

ANGEL INN, ISLINGTON TO HOLLOWAY AND HIGHBURY.

St. Mary's Church, Islington.

DRAWN & ENGRAVED BY R. JARMAN.

PUB. BY H. C. COLLINS, PATERNOSTER ROW. LONDON.

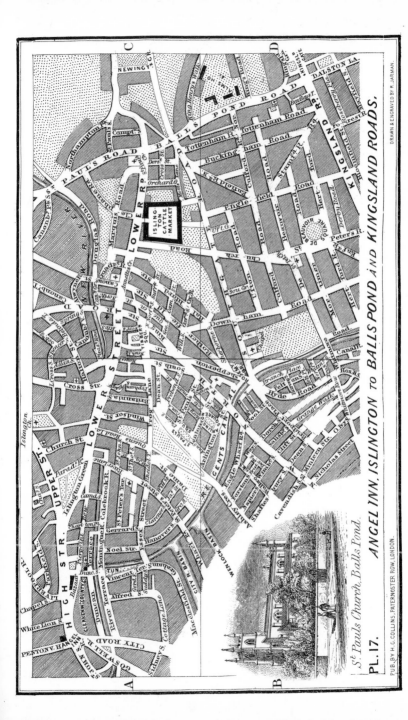

PL. 17.

ANGEL INN, ISLINGTON TO BALLS POND AND KINGSLAND ROADS.

St. Pauls Church, Balls Pond.

PUB. BY H. G. COLLINS, PATERNOSTER ROW, LONDON.

DRAWN & ENGRAVED BY R. JARMAN.

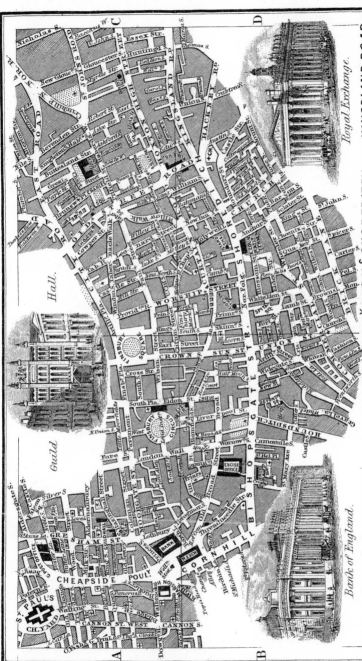

PL.18. ST PAUL'S (AND BANK) TO E. COUNTIES' RAIL.S TERM.S SHOREDITCH, AND KINGSLAND ROAD.

Royal Exchange.

Bank of England.

Hall.

Guild

PUB. BY H.C. COLLINS, PATERNOSTER ROW, LONDON.

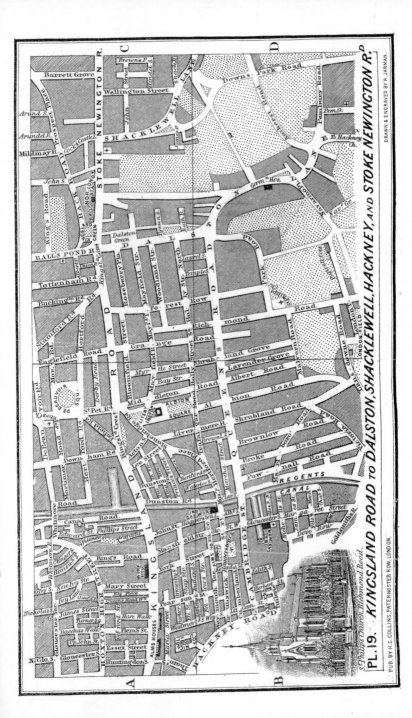

PL. 19. *KINGSLAND ROAD* to *DALSTON, SHACKLEWELL, HACKNEY, AND STOKE NEWINGTON R*ᴰ

St Philip's Church, Richmond Road.

DRAWN & ENGRAVED BY R. JARMAN.

PUB. BY H. G. COLLINS, PATERNOSTER ROW, LONDON.

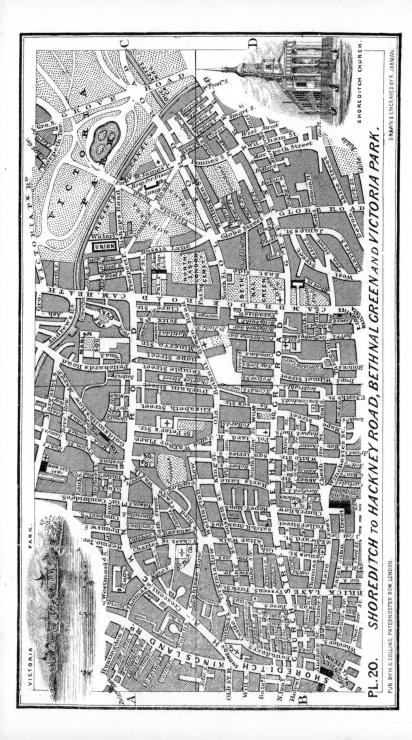

PL. 20.   SHOREDITCH TO HACKNEY ROAD, BETHNAL GREEN AND VICTORIA PARK.

VICTORIA PARK.

SHOREDITCH CHURCH.

DRAWN & ENGRAVED BY R. JARMAN.

PUB. BY H. G. COLLINS, PATERNOSTER ROW, LONDON.

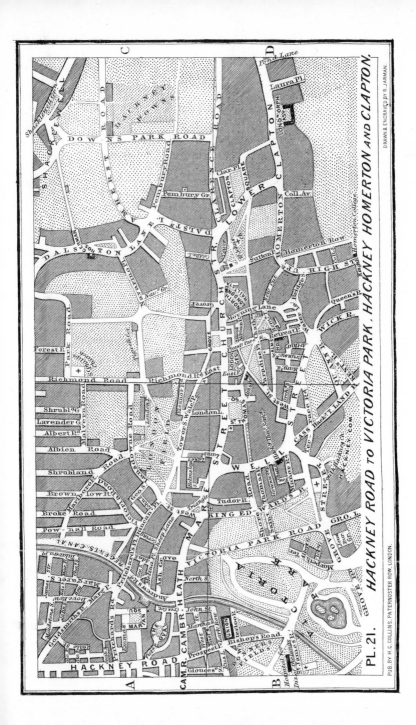

PL. 21. HACKNEY ROAD TO VICTORIA PARK, HACKNEY HOMERTON AND CLAPTON.

DRAWN & ENGRAVED BY R. JARMAN.

PUB. BY H. C. COLLINS, PATERNOSTER ROW, LONDON.

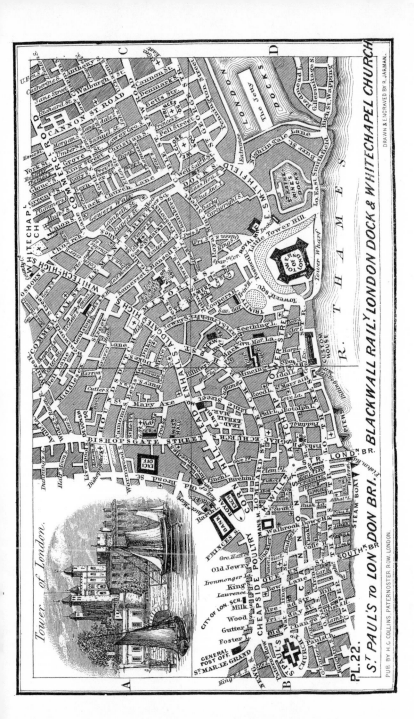

PL. 22.

ST. PAUL'S TO LONDON BRI., BLACKWALL RAILY, LONDON DOCK & WHITECHAPEL CHURCH

DRAWN & ENGRAVED BY R. JARMAN.

PUB. BY H. G. COLLINS, PATERNOSTER ROW, LONDON.

Tower of London.

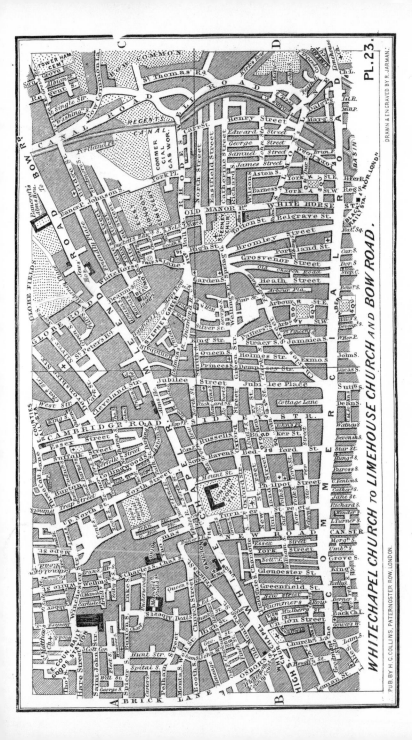

PL. 23.

DRAWN & ENGRAVED BY R. JARMAN.

WHITECHAPEL CHURCH TO LIMEHOUSE CHURCH AND BOW ROAD.

PUB. BY H. G. COLLINS, PATERNOSTER ROW, LONDON.

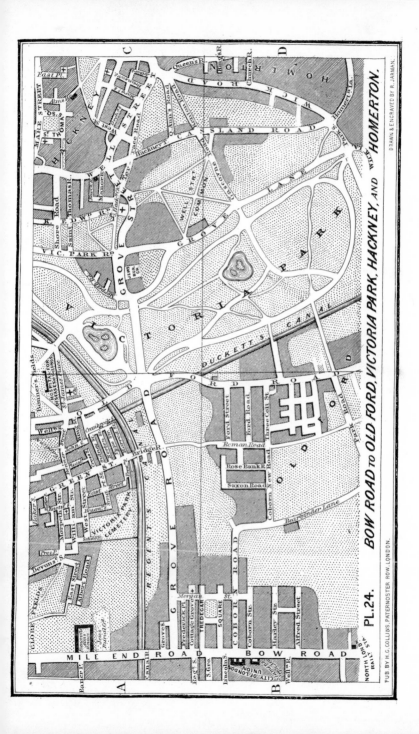

PL. 24.

BOW ROAD TO OLD FORD, VICTORIA PARK, HACKNEY, AND WICK HOMERTON.

DRAWN & ENGRAVED BY R. JARMAN.

PUB. BY H. G. COLLINS, PATERNOSTER ROW, LONDON.

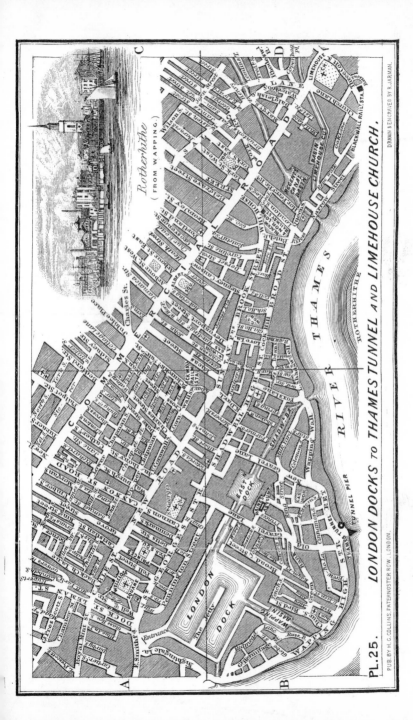

PL.25.   LONDON DOCKS TO THAMES TUNNEL AND LIMEHOUSE CHURCH.

Rotherhithe
(FROM WAPPING.)

PUB. BY H. G. COLLINS, PATERNOSTER ROW, LONDON.

DRAWN & ENGRAVED BY R. JARMAN.

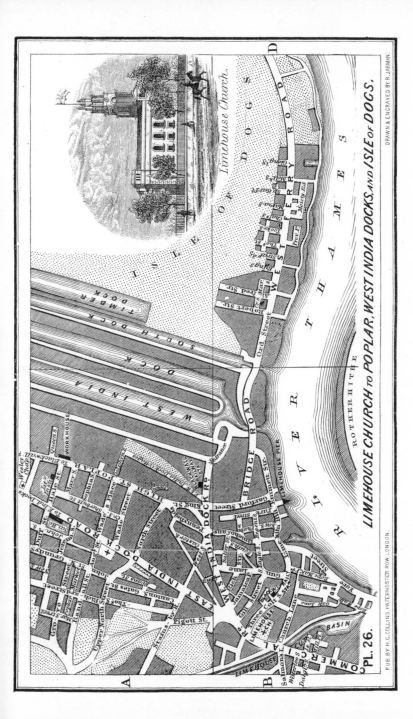

PL. 26.

LIMEHOUSE CHURCH to POPLAR, WEST INDIA DOCKS, and ISLE of DOGS.

PUB. BY H. G. COLLINS, PATERNOSTER ROW, LONDON.

DRAWN & ENGRAVED BY R. JARMAN.

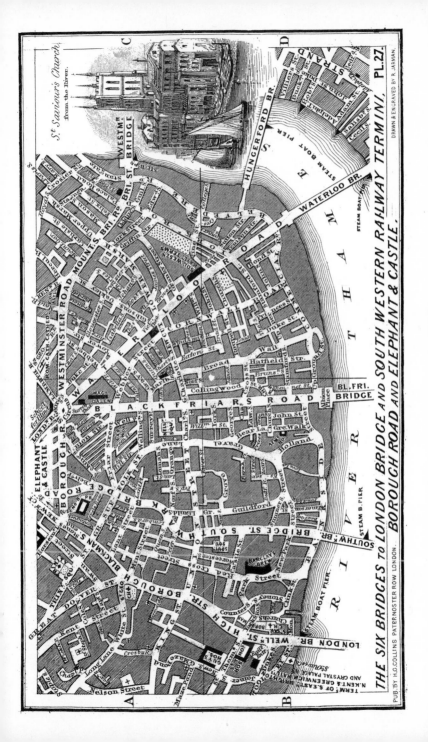

THE SIX BRIDGES to LONDON BRIDGE AND SOUTH WESTERN RAILWAY TERMINI,
BOROUGH ROAD AND ELEPHANT & CASTLE.

PL.27.

DRAWN & ENGRAVED BY R.JARMAN.

PUB. BY H.G.COLLINS PATERNOSTER ROW LONDON.

St Saviour's Church,
from the River.

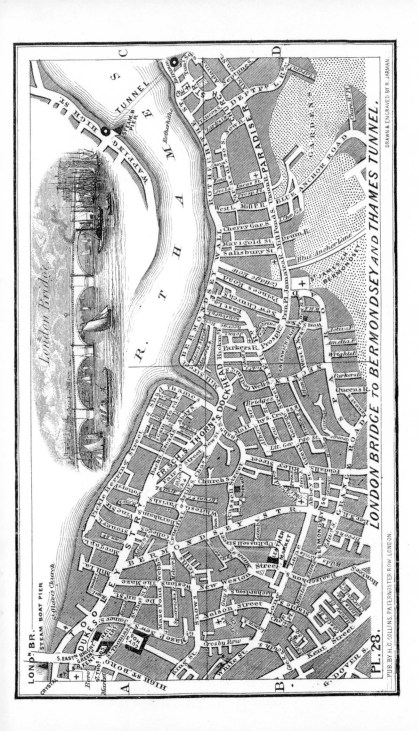

PL. 28.

LONDON BRIDGE to BERMONDSEY AND THAMES TUNNEL.

DRAWN & ENGRAVED BY R. JARMAN.

PUB. BY H.G. COLLINS, PATERNOSTER ROW, LONDON.

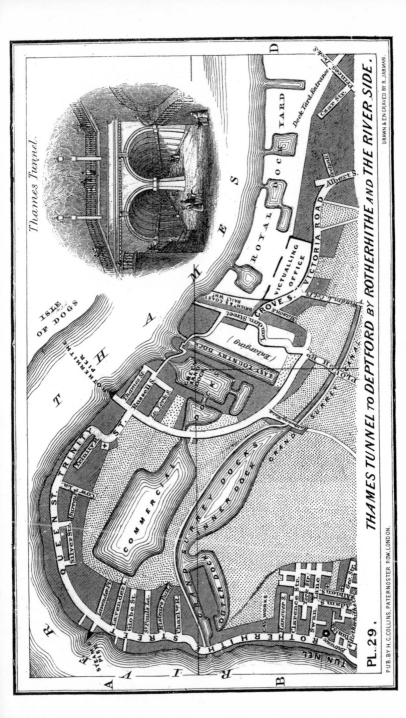

PL. 29.

Thames Tunnel.

THAMES TUNNEL TO DEPTFORD BY ROTHERHITHE AND THE RIVER SIDE.

PUB. BY H.C.COLLINS, PATERNOSTER ROW, LONDON.

DRAWN & ENGRAVED BY R. JARMAN.

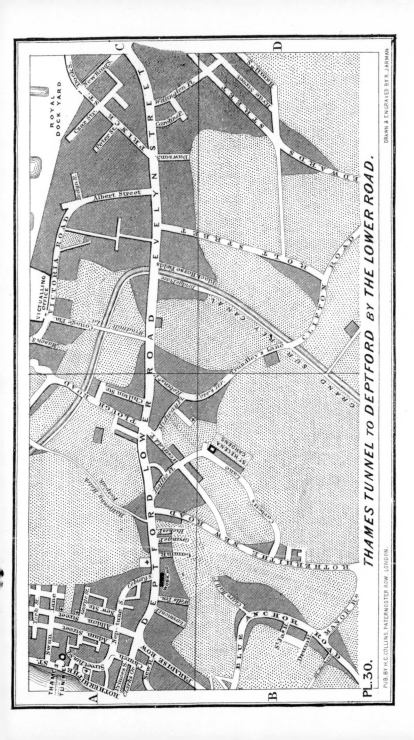

PL. 30.

THAMES TUNNEL TO DEPTFORD BY THE LOWER ROAD.

PUB. BY H.C. COLLINS, PATERNOSTER ROW LONDON.

DRAWN & ENGRAVED BY R. JARMAN.

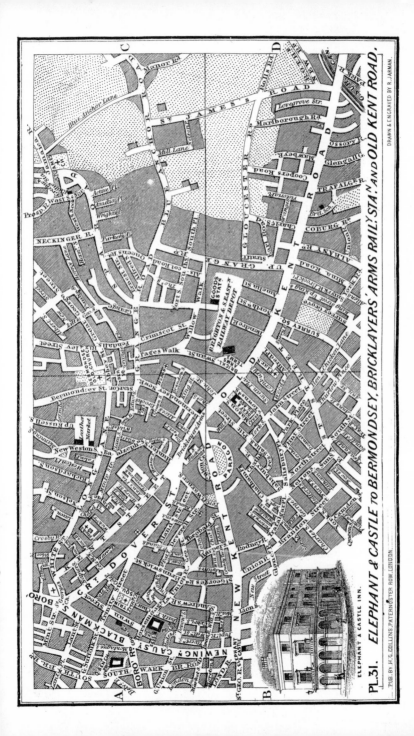

PL. 31. ELEPHANT & CASTLE TO BERMONDSEY, BRICKLAYER'S ARMS RAIL: STA:N AND OLD KENT ROAD.

ELEPHANT & CASTLE INN.

PUB. BY H.G. COLLINS PATERNOSTER ROW, LONDON.

DRAWN & ENGRAVED BY R. JARMAN.

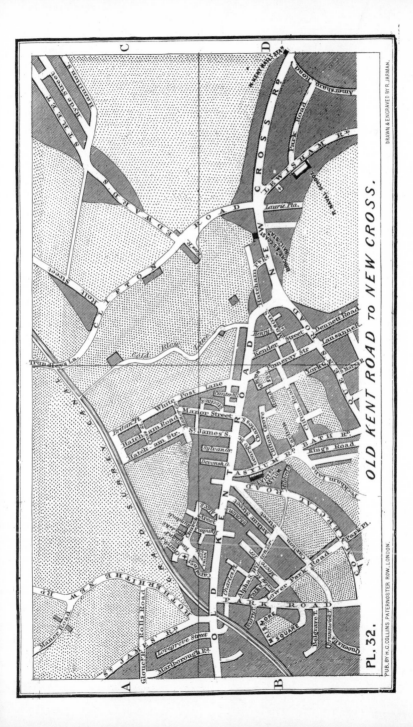

PL. 32.

OLD KENT ROAD TO NEW CROSS.

PUB. BY H. C. COLLINS, PATERNOSTER ROW, LONDON.

DRAWN & ENGRAVED BY R. JARMAN.

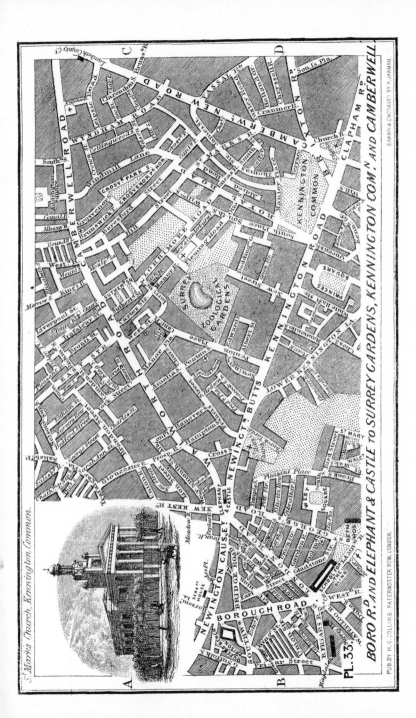

PL. 33.

BORO RD. AND ELEPHANT & CASTLE TO SURREY GARDENS, KENNINGTON COMN. AND CAMBERWELL

St Marks Church, Kennington Common.

DRAWN & ENGRAVED BY R. JARMAN.

PUB. BY H.G. COLLINS, PATERNOSTER ROW, LONDON.

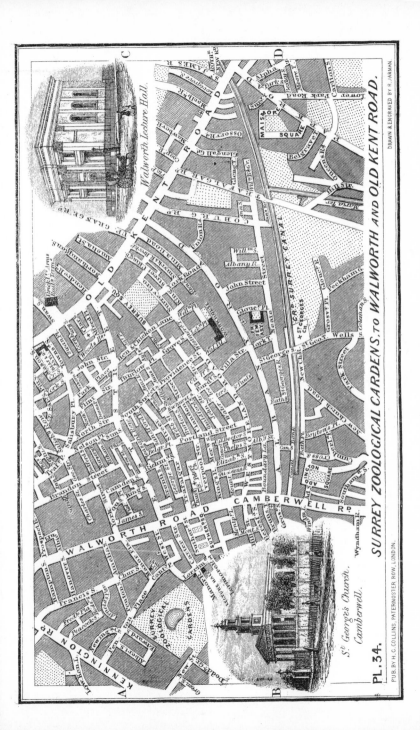

PL.34.

SURREY ZOOLOGICAL GARDENS, TO WALWORTH AND OLD KENT ROAD.

Walworth Lecture Hall.

St. George's Church, Camberwell.

DRAWN & ENGRAVED BY R. JARMAN.

PUB. BY H. G. COLLINS, PATERNOSTER ROW, LONDON.

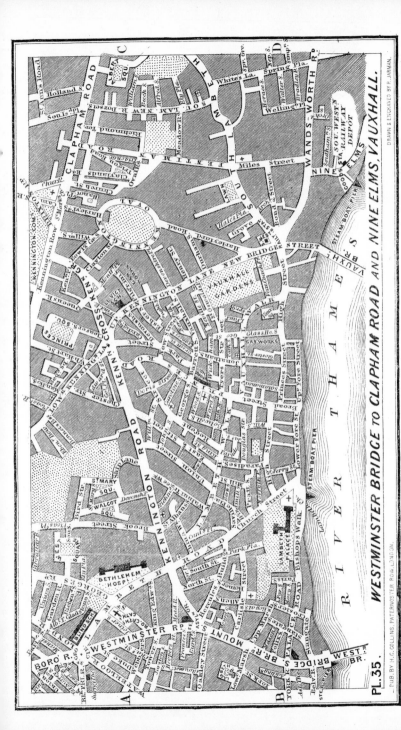

PL. 35.   WESTMINSTER BRIDGE TO CLAPHAM ROAD AND NINE ELMS, VAUXHALL.

DRAWN & ENGRAVED BY R. JARMAN.

PUB. BY H. G. COLLINS, PATERNOSTER ROW, LONDON.

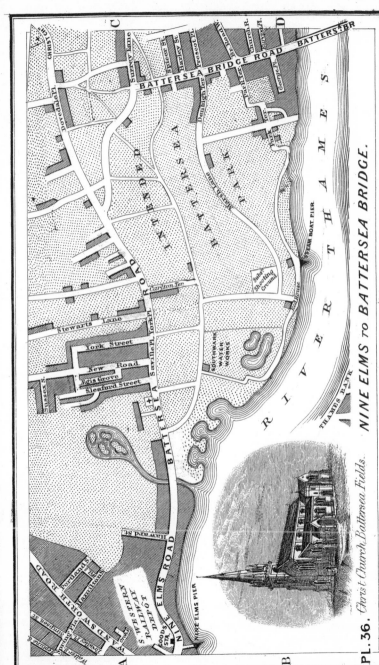

PL. 36. *Christ Church, Battersea Fields.* **NINE ELMS TO BATTERSEA BRIDGE.**

DRAWN & ENGRAVED BY R. JARMAN.

PUB. BY H.C. COLLINS, PATERNOSTER ROW, LONDON.